AI For Analogs:
A Simple, Plain-English Guide

AI For Analogs:
A Simple, Plain-English Guide

David Schippers, Sc.D.

2026 Iron Dog LLC

AI was used in editing.
Cover art and chapter art – ChatGPT

Published in the United States by Iron Dog LLC

Dave Schippers.

ISBN 978-1-972632-00-0

1.artificial intelligence, 2. human-AI collaboration, 3. AI literacy for professionals, 4. analog-to-digital transition, 5. career adaptation and reinvention, 6. future of work, 7. decision-making and judgement in AI environments, 8. AI-augmented leadership, 9. organizational culture and AI adoption, 10. cognitive resilience and adaptability, 11. prompt strategy and AI interaction, 12. AI ethics and responsibility, and 13. privacy, data protection, and AI safety.

Dedication

*To my wife Leslie-
who stood by my side
while jumping from
helicopters and
swimming with
sharks. Our
relationship is what
grounds me. Thank
you for your unending
support.*

To BE—who waited patiently as you awakened in me the call to bring truth and clarity into a world of delusion. Your guidance is the Source of this work, and may it manifest all we have envisioned.

Gate 55: The Pillars Stand –between light and shadow, the way is kept.

Table of Contents

How to Use This Book

This book was born from presenting and speaking on artificial intelligence to individuals born before 1990. As those presentations continued, it became clear that few were helping the generations with the most lived experience to understand and embrace AI. This book answers the questions that evolved from those conversations:

1. Am I too late for this — or is everyone else just moving faster than me?
2. Will AI take my job, replace my judgement, or make me obsolete?
3. How do I actually use AI without getting tricked, scammed, or misled by it?
4. What does it look like to work with AI instead of being replaced by it?
5. Will using AI change who I am — and what do I do about it?

If those questions are yours, you are in the group this book calls Analogs. Not because you are outdated. Because you built your life, your career, and your judgement before AI existed — and now you are being asked to figure out where AI fits without losing what you already know. That is a real question. This book is the honest answer.

You will find AI explained in the language you already use. Electricity. VCRs. Calculators in the classroom. Apollo. The analogies are not decoration — they are how the concepts will stay in your memory when you need them. This is the Analog approach: pattern recognition, earned judgement, and the ability to read situations that algorithms cannot.

This is not a novel. It is meant to be marked up, dog-eared, and returned to — the early chapters give you the framing you will need for translation, and the later chapters give you tools you can use this afternoon.

The prompts throughout this book are tools for immediate use. Every prompt is available as a copy-and-paste version at AIForAnalogs.com. The book teaches you how the prompts work. The website gives you the working version when you need to move fast.

At the back of the book, you will find a QR code. Scan it to obtain the free prompts, and the other companion resources built for the questions this book answers.

You already have what it takes. The rest is translation.

— Dr. Dave Schippers
Sc.D., CISSP | Founder, Iron Dog LLC

PART I

The Fear Is Normal. The Confusion Is Optional.

Chapter 1 — The New Electricity (But with Opinions)

Calvin Mercer used to light Main Street one flame at a time. Every evening, he walked the route with his ladder and pole, opening each glass lamp and touching a match to the wick. People nodded as he passed. Kids watched the quick bloom of fire. It wasn't just a job—it was a ritual, and Calvin felt like he mattered because night arrived differently when he did his work.

Then the poles went up at the edge of town. Men in heavy gloves stretched wires like tight strings, and a new kind of light appeared—white, steady, and harsh compared to gas. Folks gathered around it like it was a wild animal. Some said electricity would jump out of the air and kill you. Others said it was proof the world was turning upside down. Calvin didn't know what was true, but he knew what it felt like: the future was arriving without asking permission.

His route got shorter. A few gas lamps were replaced, then a few more. The town council posted a notice about reducing gas lighting and expanding electric service. The word "reduced" landed like a warning. At O'Rourke's Barbershop, his friends spoke the way people do when fear needs company. "It's a fad," Benny said. "It's a threat," Theo said. Calvin listened, but the fear didn't keep him warm. It just made the nights heavier.

When the supervisor finally told Calvin most lamplighter shifts would end by winter, Calvin walked home past spools of wire stacked like coiled snakes. He felt anger, then shame for feeling powerless, and then something worse…confusion. That night he told his wife, Mabel, and waited for the world to collapse. Instead, she poured coffee and said, calmly, that he had two choices: curse the wires or learn them. When Calvin muttered, he was too old, she corrected him without softness: he wasn't too old, he was scared. And scared wasn't the same thing as finished.

The next day, Calvin stepped into the power company's training shop. The tools looked foreign. The words sounded like another language: current, voltage, grounding, insulation. The first weeks humbled him. He made mistakes. He felt slow. But then he began to notice something that changed everything—electricity wasn't magic and it wasn't evil. It was structure. It was rules. It was respect. The danger wasn't electricity itself. The danger was treating it like a mystery instead of a system.

By winter, the town square glowed with electric lamps that didn't flicker in the wind. Calvin missed the warmth of flame, but he didn't miss soot in his lungs or icy rungs under his hands. When the instructor offered him paid work assisting with installs and maintenance, Calvin brought home a paycheck bigger than he'd seen in a long time. Mabel nodded once—quiet approval, like a bridge holding underweight.

Years passed and electricity spread the way grids always do: outward, steady, unstoppable. Calvin rode with crews beyond town, helping string lines toward farms that had never known a switch. In the 1930s, national efforts accelerated rural electrification through loans and cooperatives, and the countryside began to change fast. Calvin watched farmers stare at a lit bulb like it was a captured sunrise. He watched tired mothers smile at brighter kitchens. He realized he was still doing what he'd always done—bringing light—just with different tools.

One afternoon he ran into Benny outside O'Rourke's. Benny looked thinner, worn down in a way that didn't come from weather. The gasworks had cut sections and cut men, and Benny hadn't made the list. Calvin didn't gloat. He simply told him the truth: there was still time to learn, still work for people who could show up and adapt. Benny's face tightened. "I shouldn't have to," he said. Calvin nodded, because he agreed. Then he said the harder truth anyway: the world doesn't move based on what's fair. It moves based on what's next.

That night Calvin walked home under humming streetlights and felt something he hadn't felt the day he lost his route: control. Not control over change, just control over his response to it.

Electricity hadn't just replaced his old job. It had given him a better one, but only after he stopped treating the grid like an enemy and started treating it like a skill. The future didn't reward the loudest complainers. It rewarded the first learners.

Same Disruption, Different Current

When electricity first arrived in homes and cities, people didn't celebrate. They worried it would kill them. They feared fires. They assumed it would wipe out whole jobs built around candles, oil lamps, and gaslight. Some of those fears were exaggerated, but the emotional reaction wasn't foolish. It was the normal response humans have when the world changes faster than their habits can keep up.

And the truth is: electricity really did disrupt everything. It didn't politely "add on" to life the way a new kitchen gadget does. It rewired the entire system. It changed how streets looked at night. It changed how factories ran. It changed how long businesses could stay open. It moved work from one kind of labor to another. It made some skills less valuable, and made new skills priceless.

Then, after the fear and the disruption, electricity did something bigger than anyone expected. It became the foundation under everything that came after. Refrigeration changed food and health. Radios changed culture. Assembly lines changed the economy. Elevators changed cities. Air conditioning changed where people could live and how they could work. Computers changed information itself. Electricity wasn't just a tool. It became the grid beneath modern life.

AI is moving into that same role. AI is becoming a kind of grid—something you plug into without always thinking about it. But there's a twist. This grid talks back. It makes suggestions. It nudges. It can sound calm, smart, and sure of itself. That makes it feel less like a machine and more like a presence.

So, AI is the new electricity. The question is not whether you will use it. The question is whether you know where the switches are.

AI feels different than past technology waves for a few reasons, and none of them are science fiction. First, it's moving faster than most people can adjust. Electricity took decades to spread. Telephones took decades. Computers took decades. Even the Internet—though it moved quickly—still took years before it became the default for daily life. AI is spreading in months. It shows up in your email, your phone, your search, your camera, your customer service, your banking, and your workplace tools. You don't "buy AI" as one thing. You discover it has already been installed in the things you use.

Second, AI uses language. That sounds simple, but it's a big deal. Nobody thought their toaster was alive. Nobody thought the fax machine had a personality. But when something writes full sentences, answers questions, and sounds polite, the human brain automatically shifts gears. We're wired to treat language like a sign of mind. We hear a voice—even a written voice—and we start to treat the source like a someone, not a something. That is the trap. AI can sound human without being human.

Third, AI can feel less neutral than older technology. Electricity didn't argue with you. It didn't steer your attention. It didn't offer a "recommended next step." It simply powered whatever you chose to do. AI often works by predicting what you might want next and giving you an output that feels like advice. This is why AI can feel like it has "opinions." Not because it has beliefs or a soul, but because it is built to guess what response will satisfy the prompt. It's not trying to be moral. It's trying to be useful. Those are not the same thing.

That leads to the most important truth in this chapter: AI is not a thinking being. AI is a prediction engine. If you remember only one sentence, remember that one.

A prediction engine looks at patterns in huge amounts of information and predicts what comes next. You've already lived with prediction engines for years. Your phone predicts the next word when you text. Netflix predicts what you'll want to watch next. Your GPS predicts the fastest route. Spam filters predict what's junk mail. Credit card systems predict what might be fraud. AI is that same basic idea, scaled up dramatically and applied to language, images, and planning.

A helpful way to picture it is "supercharged autocomplete." Autocomplete doesn't understand your life. It doesn't have values. It doesn't know what matters to you. It just guesses the next likely word based on patterns. AI does the same thing, but with full paragraphs, outlines, emails, summaries, and suggestions. It can feel like thinking because it produces the kinds of outputs we associate with thinking. But producing a convincing answer is not the same as understanding.

This is why AI can be impressive and still be wrong. It can write something that sounds confident and polished while the foundation underneath is shaky. It can stitch together information in a way that looks smooth but includes errors. It can even make up details that sound realistic. When people talk about AI "hallucinating," that's just a technical way of saying the system predicted an answer that fits the shape of the question—even if it doesn't match reality.

So, the goal is not to "trust AI" or "fear AI." The goal is to use AI with judgement. Electricity became safe and useful when people learned the basics: grounding, fuses, breakers, wattage, and not sticking a fork in a socket. The same kind of practical literacy is what makes AI safe and useful.

Most people fall into three predictable mistakes when they meet AI: myth, panic, and over trust.

The first mistake is myth. Myth sounds like, "AI is alive," or "AI is conscious," or "AI is about to become a god," or "AI understands me." Myth turns AI into magic. Sometimes it becomes worship. Sometimes it becomes horror. Either way, it takes you out of reality. AI doesn't have life experience. It doesn't have a conscience. It doesn't have wisdom. It doesn't "want" anything. It predicts. Myth makes people waste energy fighting ghosts or following a machine like it's a prophet.

The second mistake is panic. Panic sounds like, "This will replace everyone," or "This will destroy all jobs," or "There's nothing I can do." Panic is understandable because disruption is real. Electricity did replace jobs. So did factories. So did computers. So did self-checkout. So did online banking. But the pattern is also consistent: disruption shifts work. It doesn't erase human usefulness. It changes what becomes valuable.

In an AI world, what becomes more valuable is not memorizing more facts. Facts are cheap now. What becomes more valuable is judgement, communication, verification, leadership, and problem-solving. People who can ask better questions, check outputs, spot errors, understand consequences, and make decisions will matter more, not less. Panic freezes people in place. AI punishes freezing, because the world doesn't pause while you decide how you feel about it.

The third mistake is over trust, and it's the most dangerous. Over trust sounds like, "If the AI said it, it must be true," or "It wrote it, so I can submit it," or "It sounds confident, so it's correct." Confidence is not accuracy. A smooth answer is not a verified answer. Over trust is how bad information gets sent to customers, how fake sources end up in reports, and how organizations make decisions based on outputs nobody checked. If panic is paralysis, over trust is reckless speed.

If AI is the new grid, then "knowing where the switches are" means building simple habits that keep you in control. You don't need to be a programmer. You need to be the adult in the room.

The first switch is deciding what AI is allowed to do and what it is not allowed to do. AI is excellent at drafting, summarizing, brainstorming, organizing, creating options, and helping you get unstuck. It is not excellent at being your final authority for medical, legal, financial, or safety decisions. The rule of thumb that works for most people is this: let AI do the first 80%, but you do the last 20%. That last 20% is where truth, tone, context, and consequences live.

The second switch is demanding sources and checking them. If AI gives you a "fact," ask where it came from. Ask for citations. Ask for links. Then verify. This is not being paranoid. This is being responsible. Electricity required basic safety steps. AI requires basic verification steps.

The third switch is treating AI like a junior assistant, not a senior expert. A junior assistant can be fast and helpful, but you still review their work. You still correct mistakes. You still decide what goes out the door with your name on it. This mindset protects you from over trust without dragging you into fear.

The fourth switch is keeping humans in the loop. AI is strong at producing outputs. Humans are strong at meaning, ethics, empathy, and understanding what actually matters in a specific situation. Humans understand consequences. Humans understand when the "right answer" is still the wrong move. If AI starts steering decisions without a human checking, you don't have innovation—you have a slow-motion accident.

This chapter isn't asking you to become a tech person. It's asking you to become a switch-flipper. Electricity didn't ask permission. It arrived. People who learned it gained power—literally and financially. People who refused it didn't stop the grid. They just got left in the dark.

AI is arriving the same way. It will disrupt. It will replace some tasks. It will elevate others. It will power what comes next. So, stop arguing about whether AI is "good" or "bad" like it's a political issue. Start asking a better question: where are my switches?

Because the people who win in this world won't be the people with the loudest opinions about AI. They'll be the people who can use it without being used by it.

Chapter 2 — Is This Going to Take My Job?

In the 1980s, when ATMs started showing up everywhere, a lot of people thought bank tellers were finished. Economists made confident predictions that machines would replace humans, and that the teller job would disappear. On the surface, it made sense. ATMs could hand out cash, take deposits, and run simple transactions without needing a person behind a counter.

But something surprising happened. Banks didn't shrink. They grew. More branches opened, not fewer. More transactions flowed through the system, not less. And instead of killing the teller job, ATMs changed it. The teller role shifted away from counting bills and stamping deposit slips. It shifted toward helping customers solve real problems—fixing account mistakes, handling disputes, explaining fees, helping with loans, and building relationships. The tellers who insisted their value was only "cash handling" got replaced. The tellers who moved into customer problem-solving became more valuable than before.

Same disruption. Two completely different outcomes. The difference wasn't the ATM. The difference was what the tellers decided their identity was. If their identity was "I count money," the machine won. If their identity was "I help people solve problems," the machine became a tool, not a threat.

So, as you read the rest of Chapter 2, keep the ATM story in your mind. The question is not only "Will AI change work?" It will. The question is: which part of your work is routine, and which part is human value—judgement, problem-solving, and trust? The future belongs to the people who shift toward the part a machine can't truly own.

The First Question

The first question most people ask about AI isn't philosophical. It's personal. "Is this going to take my job?" That question isn't silly, and it isn't weak. It's what a serious person asks when they've spent years building skill, reliability, and a reputation. If you've lived long enough to watch whole industries change—factories automating, self-checkout spreading, phone calls turning into email, and paper turning into screens—you already know the pattern. Big technology waves don't ask permission. They arrive, they spread, and they rewrite what "normal work" looks like.

But we need to be honest: the fear isn't only about paychecks. The deeper threat is identity. For a lot of Analogs, work wasn't just what you did. It was part of who you were. You became "the person who knows." You were the one people called when something broke, when a decision needed wisdom, when a team needed steadiness. AI doesn't just threaten jobs. It threatens the feeling of being valuable because you mastered something.

In this book, when I say **Analogs**, I mean people born before 1990—people who remember life before the Internet was everywhere. You remember the world when you could not instantly Google an answer. You remember using paper, face-to-face conversations, and learning by doing. Many Analogs became **Digital Immigrants** over time. You didn't grow up with the digital world, but you moved into it. You learned email, apps, online banking, and passwords like adults learn anything new: with effort, patience, and sometimes frustration. You adapted, even if you didn't love every part of it.

Digital Natives, usually people born after 1990, grew up with digital tools from early childhood. Screens, search engines, texting, and social media were normal before they were teenagers. For them, digital wasn't something they "added." It was the environment.

Now here's the twist: **every person alive today is an AI Immigrant.** Even Digital Natives. AI did not grow up with us. We are all learning it in real time. Some people will learn faster, and some will resist longer, but no one gets to say, "I was born fluent in this." That's good news, because it means there is no shame in being new. This is a doorway we are all walking through together.

The real shift AI brings is not "jobs disappearing overnight." The real shift is that work moves from **routine execution** to **adaptive problem solving**. Routine execution is work that follows the same steps again and again: writing the standard email, filling out the standard form, summarizing the standard meeting, answering the same customer questions, and producing the same monthly report with the same structure. That work is still important, but it is the easiest for AI to speed up, because AI is built to find patterns and repeat them quickly.

Adaptive problem solving is different. It shows up when the customer doesn't fit the normal case, when the numbers don't add up, when the team is stuck, when risk is hidden, or when the situation changes in the middle. Adaptive work is messy. It depends on context. It requires judgement. It requires experience and awareness. AI can help in those moments, but it usually cannot fully own them, because it doesn't truly understand consequences the way humans do.

This is where people get confused about AI. Some see it as **automation**. Others see it as **amplification**. Automation means the machine replaces the task.

Amplification means the machine multiplies the human. If you've ever used a power tool, you understand amplification. A drill doesn't replace a carpenter. It replaces the slowest part of the carpenter's day. It saves time and reduces strain, but the carpenter still chooses what to build, checks measurements, and takes responsibility for the final result.

Used well, AI is an amplifier. It can draft a first version, summarize information, generate options when you're stuck, organize a messy set of notes, and help you move faster from idea to output. That isn't replacement. That's leverage. But there's a catch: when the first draft becomes cheap, the skill of "making the first draft" becomes less valuable. What becomes more valuable is shaping the draft, checking it, improving it, and making sure it fits reality. AI changes what counts as skill, and that's why it feels like the ground is shifting.

Now we need to name the part most books skip.

The Grief Nobody Talks About

Nobody wants to admit this part out loud. People will talk about job loss and automation because that feels practical and safe to discuss. But there is a quieter pain underneath, and it hits Analogs the hardest. It isn't only fear of being replaced. It is the grief of watching your hard-earned mastery get treated like it's optional.

Mark was 58 and had been doing his job for thirty years. In his world—policies, compliance reviews, risk reports—he wasn't flashy, but he was trusted. When things were unclear, people called Mark. When leaders needed a straight answer without drama, they called Mark. He earned that role the slow way: years of experience, mistakes, lessons, and results.

One Monday morning, Mark sat in a conference room while a junior colleague named Jenna opened her laptop. Jenna was smart and hardworking, but she didn't have Mark's depth yet. She hadn't lived through past failures. She hadn't learned what goes wrong when one sentence is worded the wrong way, or when a "small" risk is ignored until it becomes a headline.

The manager said, "We need a first draft of the annual risk summary by end of day." Mark almost laughed. That report used to take a week. Not because he was slow, but because it required specialized knowledge—how to write it so legal wouldn't panic, how to frame it so executives would actually read it, and how to tell the truth without starting a political fire.

Jenna nodded, opened an AI tool, typed a prompt, and pasted in a few bullet points. In minutes, the screen filled with clean, organized paragraphs that looked a lot like what Mark had spent years learning to write. Twenty minutes later, Jenna said, "Here's a draft. I'll refine it."

Mark didn't feel jealous. He wasn't angry at Jenna. He didn't hate the tool. He felt grief. Not because the draft was perfect, but because it looked "good enough" to people who didn't know what good really costs.

If you are an Analog, you may have built your identity around mastery. You became good at something through years of effort. You learned the hard way. You earned trust. You earned status. You became "the one who knows how to do the thing." And there is a quiet pride in that. It is not arrogance. It is the dignity of competence.

AI can feel like it spits on that dignity. Because suddenly, a machine can do a version of your work in seconds. Suddenly, the thing that took you ten years to master can be imitated by someone who just knows how to type a prompt. Suddenly, the world looks like it might value speed over wisdom, and output over understanding.

If that makes you feel angry, you're not broken. If it makes you feel sad, you're not weak. If it makes you feel like the world is disrespecting your life experience, that is not you being dramatic. That is grief.

It is grief for expertise that may be devalued. It is grief for a role you carried with pride. It is grief for the old rules: "Work hard, get good, and you will always be needed." Do not rush past that grief. Do not let anyone mock it. And do not talk yourself out of it with fake positivity. You can respect the grief and still move forward. In fact, you must. Because grief is not the end of the story. It is the signal that something meaningful is changing.

Now we need to separate two things people confuse: expertise and wisdom. **Expertise** is the ability to produce the right output inside a known system. It's writing the report, following the process, creating the deliverable, and doing it reliably. AI can devalue parts of that kind of mastery, especially the parts that are routine and repeatable. If work has a pattern, AI can learn the pattern and copy it fast.

Wisdom is different. Wisdom is context. Wisdom is consequence awareness. Wisdom is knowing when the "correct" answer is still the wrong move. Wisdom is understanding the human terrain—trust, history, politics, risk, and what happens after the document leaves the room. AI can imitate the shape of expertise. It cannot live the weight of wisdom.

This is where an old maxim fit—what I call the Samurai lesson. A truly dangerous person is not the one who can do something once. A truly dangerous person is the one who knows what **not** to do. And you only learn what not to do by making mistakes, surviving them, and remembering the cost. If you have never made the mistakes, you don't know the landmines. You don't know the edge cases. You don't know the shortcuts that look smart until they break something important.

AI doesn't have scars. It can produce a clean draft without any sense of danger. It can sound confident without understanding consequences. That's why it can be helpful and risky at the same time. It will hand you an answer that looks strong, but it cannot tell you if that answer will survive contact with real life.

Here is the reframe: AI is not only changing what the world needs. It is changing where mastery lives. In the old world, mastery often meant perfect execution. Do the steps. Do them well. Do them every time. In the AI world, mastery shifts upward. It becomes the ability to ask the right questions, spot the wrong answers, and make good decisions when the output looks convincing but the stakes are real. It becomes the ability to connect the work to meaning, ethics, and consequences. It becomes the ability to lead humans through uncertainty, not just complete tasks.

In other words, the mastery doesn't disappear. It moves.

And the people best prepared for that shift are often the ones who already understand responsibility, tradeoffs, and real-world consequences. That's not a "young person skill." That's a lived-experience skill.

This is also where the most important practical reassurance belongs. Humans still dominate in three areas that AI cannot replace in any real way: judgement, accountability, and meaning. Judgement is knowing what matters, what is risky, what is missing, and what is false—even when it sounds confident. Accountability is ownership. When something goes wrong, a human being is still responsible. AI cannot take the blame, fix trust, or repair damage. **Meaning** is purpose and story. People don't follow plans just because they are efficient. They commit when it matters. AI can produce words about meaning, but it cannot truly care, and it cannot carry moral weight.

Now return to Mark and Jenna. The AI draft Jenna produced might be useful, but without Mark, it might also be dangerous. Mark knows what questions to ask because he knows what matters. Mark can spot what's missing because he knows where things fail. Mark can predict consequences because he has watched consequences happen. Without that filter, the output is just noise dressed up as confidence.

This is the shift most people miss: in the AI era, your thirty years of experience did not become worthless. It became premium input. It became the filter everyone else needs. The first draft is cheaper and faster now, but the ability to judge, correct, and protect becomes more valuable. AI will punish routine and reward adaptation. If your identity was built only on doing routine work well, you will feel threatened. If your identity can expand into sensemaking, decision-making, and leadership, you will become more valuable, not less.

So don't ask only, "Will AI take my job?" Ask the better question: "What part of my mastery can AI never truly own?" Then build there. That's not denial. That's strategy.

Your experience did not become worthless. It became the filter everyone else needs.

Chapter 3 — AI in Plain English: A 10-Minute Mental Model

Calvin liked the library because it still ran on silence and paper. No rumors, no barroom certainty—just oak tables, old pages, and facts that didn't care how loud you were. On a gray afternoon, he walked in with a simple goal: learn electricity the right way, not through fear stories.

The card catalog sat like a wooden machine full of tiny drawers. Calvin pulled one open and scanned the neat cards: *circuits, wiring, safety, grounding*. He was still getting used to the idea that answers could be found instead of guessed.

"Looking for something specific?" Mrs. Ellery asked from behind the desk. She was the reference librarian—small, sharp-eyed, and famous for "knowing everything." Calvin told her he wanted real information about electricity, especially safety. She nodded like this was the most normal thing in the world, then moved to the catalog and flipped through cards with calm speed. In seconds, she handed him a stack of call numbers and pointed him toward the right shelves.

Calvin spent the next hour reading. The language was technical, but it wasn't mystical. It was rules and cause-and-effect. The more he read, the less electricity felt like a monster and the more it felt like a system you could respect and control.

When he brought a book back with a question, Mrs. Ellery answered quickly—so quickly it felt like she had the whole library stored in her head. Then she added one detail with complete confidence, a number she stated like it was carved in stone. Calvin paused, because it didn't match what he'd just read. He didn't argue. He went back to his table and checked the page. The correct number was slightly different.

Mrs. Ellery had misremembered a detail.

Calvin sat with that for a moment, then smiled to himself. He wasn't going to stop using the librarian. She was still incredibly valuable. She could guide him, save him time, and point him to the right sources faster than he ever could alone. He just learned the rule that mattered: use the helper for speed and direction, but verify the facts that carry weight.

Walking out into the cold, Calvin realized he'd just learned something bigger than electricity. A tool—or a helper—doesn't have to be perfect to be useful. The key is knowing which parts you can trust for momentum, and which parts you must check before you build anything real.

Comprehending AI Technology in Plain English

Most people don't fear AI because it's "too smart." They fear it because it feels unclear. When you don't understand what a tool is doing, you either avoid it or you treat it like magic. Neither one helps you. This chapter is here to give you a simple mental picture of what AI is and what it is not—so you can use it without being fooled by it.

Here's the plainest definition that actually works: modern AI is a machine that learned patterns from a huge number of examples, and it uses those patterns to predict what should come next. That's the core of it. Not a brain. Not a person. Not a thinking creature hiding inside a computer. It's a prediction engine that got really good at language.

This is important because prediction can look like thinking. If a system predicts the right next word again and again, it can produce sentences that sound human. If it predicts the right next sentence again and again, it can produce paragraphs that sound like an expert. But sounding human is not the same as understanding. AI can sound like it "knows" when it is really just matching patterns.

To understand AI, you only need three ideas: training data, patterns, and probabilities. Training data is what the AI learned from. Think of it like a giant warehouse full of examples. Not one bookshelf. Not one room. A warehouse. The AI "studies" that warehouse and learns how language usually works—how people ask questions, how answers usually look, what kinds of words tend to go together, and what a "good response" sounds like in different situations.

Patterns are the repeated shapes inside the warehouse. Here's an easy example. If you read thousands of recipes, you start to see patterns. Recipes usually begin with ingredients, then steps. They often include phrases like "preheat the oven," "stir until," and "serve warm." You don't have to be a chef to predict what comes next in a recipe. After enough examples, the structure becomes familiar. AI does something similar, but with writing, emails, reports, instructions, and conversations.

Probabilities are how AI makes its next move. It's constantly making a guess: "Given what came before, what is the most likely next word?" Then it does that again. And again. Like a weather forecast, it isn't guessing randomly. It's predicting based on patterns. A forecast looks at conditions and says, "Rain is likely." AI looks at words and says, "This next word is likely." When it keeps doing that quickly and smoothly, it can produce a full answer.

That leads to the best everyday metaphor for AI: it's like super-autocomplete with research assistant energy. You've seen autocomplete on your phone. You type "See you" and it suggests "soon." That's tiny prediction. AI is the same basic idea, but stronger. It can take your half-formed thought and produce a whole email. It can take a question and produce an outline. It can take messy notes and turn them into something organized.

The "research assistant energy" part is why people get confused. AI can summarize information fast. It can compare options. It can pull together a list of ideas. It can make a plan. That feels like research, because it saves you time and gives you structure. And it can be genuinely helpful that way. But you should not confuse speed with truth. A real research assistant can say, "I don't know," and then go check sources carefully. AI often does not do that unless you ask it to.

This is where the most important warning comes in: AI can be confidently wrong. You will hear people call this "hallucination." That word sounds dramatic, but the idea is simple. A hallucination happens when AI generates an answer that fits the shape of the question, but the answer is not tied down to reality.

Machine or Human Hallucinations?

AI gets mocked for "hallucinating," which means it can give a confident answer that is wrong. That makes people laugh, and it makes headlines, because it feels like proof the machine can't be trusted. But there is a harder truth hiding under that joke. Humans hallucinate too. We do it any time we speak with certainty without evidence. We do it when we assume, guess, or repeat something we heard, and then treat it like fact.

I've sat in rooms full of smart, confident leaders who said their teams were doing great. They sounded certain. They sounded polished. But they had no proof. No metrics. No data. No audits. Just feelings and confidence. That kind of leadership isn't leadership. It's speculation. And in a world where decisions affect real systems and real people, lazy thinking turns into real damage.

This is why AI hallucinations matter. They are not just a "machine problem." They are a mirror. When AI makes up a source, it looks like the human habit of repeating headlines without reading. When AI gives a believable answer that is untrue, it looks like the human habit of speaking from ego instead of evidence. When AI fails to separate facts from guesses, it exposes how often people do the same thing without noticing.

The lesson is not to fear AI or mock it. The lesson is to build better thinking habits. In cyber work, we learn early that "no evidence found" does not mean "nothing is there." It often means we didn't look hard enough or ask the right questions. The same rule applies to everyday decisions. If we don't test our beliefs, we end up running on assumptions. And assumptions, when they are dressed up as confidence, become operational risks.

So, here is the simple takeaway for Analogs: the answer isn't perfect AI. The answer is stronger human judgement. That means practicing intellectual humility. It means being willing to say, "I don't know," and then finding out. It means checking sources, asking for evidence, and slowing down when confidence shows up without proof. In the age of AI, discernment is not optional. It is the firewall that protects you from machine errors and from human delusion.

Imagine you ask a coworker, "What time is the meeting?" If they didn't check, a careful person would say, "I'm not sure—let me look." A reckless person might say, "It's at 3:00," because 3:00 sounds believable. They're not trying to hurt you. They just want to sound helpful and keep the conversation moving. That's the problem. AI has the same weakness, but with cleaner grammar and a calmer tone.

This is why AI can invent things that sound real. It might create a quote that nobody said. It might give a statistic that sounds right but has no source. It might name a law, a policy, or a book that doesn't exist. It might mix up dates, places, and people. It might take a real idea and fill in the missing parts with guesses. If you don't check it, you can end up repeating fiction with confidence.

So why does AI do this? Because it is built to generate a response, not to protect you from mistakes. It's trained to be useful, smooth, and responsive. When it doesn't have a strong anchor for the answer, it will still produce something that sounds plausible. Again, that's not evil. That's how prediction works. Prediction is not the same thing as truth.

The good news is you can catch most hallucinations with a few simple habits. Think of these habits like the safety rules people learned with electricity. Electricity is powerful, but you don't treat it like magic. You learn the basics and you respect it.

The first habit is to watch for answers that are "too clean." Real life is messy. Real experts often say, "It depends," or "Here's what I know," or "Here's the source." If an answer sounds perfect, complete, and absolutely certain about something that normally requires checking—slow down. That is a risk signal.

The second habit is to demand sources when facts matter. If AI gives you a claim about a law, a medical issue, a policy, a historical event, or a number, ask, "Where did that come from?" Ask for links, citations, or document names. If it cannot give you anything you can check, treat the answer like a draft, not like a fact.

The third habit is to verify the load-bearing parts. You do not need to check every word. Check the beams that hold the building up: names, dates, quotes, numbers, and official rules. If those are wrong, the whole answer can collapse.

The fourth habit is to use the "what would disagree?" question. Ask, "What is the counterargument?" or "What are the limits of this answer?" When AI is bluffing, it often struggles to show the other side clearly. When it is grounded, it can usually provide balanced tradeoffs.

The fifth habit is the simplest and maybe the best: the "would I bet money on this?" test. If you would not bet money on the claim, don't bet your reputation on it either. Use AI to get started, but don't outsource responsibility.

Now let's land this plane. AI is powerful, but it is not mystical. It learned patterns from a huge pile of examples, and it predicts what comes next. That is why it can write fast. That is why it can sound smart. That is why it can be confidently wrong.

For Analogs, the advantage is clear. Do not compete with AI on speed. Compete on judgement. AI can generate words, but you still decide what is true, what matters, what is safe, and what should happen next. That last part—meaning, responsibility, and consequence—is still human territory.

Chapter 4 — The AI Spectrum: Dumb Tools, Smart Partners and Safety

It's 1985. You walk into a typical Baby Boomer or Gen X house, and you can tell a lot about the family just by the sounds coming from the walls.

In the kitchen, there's a small transistor AM radio on the counter. It does one thing: it plays the station you tune in. You might turn the volume knob, maybe twist the dial a little, but that's about it. It's simple. It's predictable. If it sounds bad, you move the antenna or change the station. Nobody worries the radio will "do something" on its own. It can't.

Down the hall, a teenager has a Walkman clipped to their belt. It's personal. It's portable. It's not just "radio"—it's choice. You can pick what you listen to. You can rewind your favorite song and play it again. You can make a mixtape and bring your own world with you. The Walkman feels smarter than the kitchen radio because it starts to shape your attention. It follows your taste. It makes it easy to keep listening to what you already like.

Then you step into the living room, and that's where the serious system is. A component hi-fi setup sits like a spaceship: turntable, receiver, equalizer, and big speakers that look like they could shake the furniture loose. It can sound amazing, but it also demands respect. You have to know what each piece does. You have to know which cables go where. You have to understand power and balance. If you wire it wrong or crank it too hard, you don't just get "bad sound." You can blow a speaker. You can fry a component. The more sophisticated the system, the more it can do—and the more you need to know to use it safely.

That spectrum maps directly onto AI.

The kitchen radio is like a basic search engine. You ask a question, you get results, and you decide what to do with them. It's limited, and it mostly "points" instead of "acts."

The Walkman is like a recommendation algorithm. It doesn't just respond to what you ask. It tries to guess what you'll want next. It nudges your attention toward certain choices. Most of the time it's convenient, but over time it can box you in without you noticing.

And the component hi-fi system—where you can accidentally blow your speakers if you run too much power through the wrong setup—is like an AI agent. Agents don't just answer questions. They can take actions. They can send messages, schedule things, move files, and trigger steps in real systems. When an agent is wrong, the consequences are real, because something might already be done.

That's the safety lesson of Chapter 4 in one picture: the smarter the tool gets, the more it needs supervision. Dumb tools do exactly what you tell them. Smart partners can help you—but they can also amplify mistakes if you don't know how the pieces connect. In the AI era, your job isn't to fear the equipment. Your job is to learn the knobs, the wiring, and the limits—so you get great sound without blowing up the system.

That's the point of this chapter: know what kind of tool you're using. The smarter it feels, the more you need your brain turned on.

Know What You're Dealing With — Then Deal with It

AI isn't one thing, and that's the first mistake most people make. Marketing loves to say "AI" the way a car dealer says "performance." It sounds powerful, but it doesn't tell you what you're really getting. Some AI tools are basically smarter search bars. Some are recommendation engines that nudge your attention. Some are copilots that help you write and plan. And some are agents that can actually take actions for you. The farther you move along that spectrum, the more helpful the tool can become—and the more it can hurt you if you don't understand what it's doing.

Search is the simplest place to start. You type a question and get results. It doesn't feel like a "partner." It feels like a tool. The important part is that search usually shows its work by giving you links. You can open the source and decide if it's trustworthy. Search can still be biased, and it can still rank junk ahead of truth, but at least you can see where the information came from.

Recommendation is different. It doesn't wait for you to ask. It guesses what you want next and pushes it toward you. Netflix, YouTube, Amazon, and social media do this all day long. Recommendation systems can be convenient, but they also shape what you notice, what you believe is "normal," and what you spend time on. They don't just respond to your preferences. Over time, they train your preferences.

Copilots are where AI starts to feel like a teammate. This is the world of ChatGPT-style tools. You ask a question, give it a prompt, or paste in a rough draft, and it helps you produce something: an email, a summary, a plan, an outline, a list of options, or a first draft that gets you past the blank page. This is extremely useful, but it comes with one important rule: a copilot is not an expert. It's a fast assistant. It can be right, and it can be wrong, and it can sound calm either way. That's why copilots work best when you use them for speed and structure, then you verify the facts that matter.

Agents are the next step, and this is where the stakes jump. An agent doesn't just help you write or think. An agent can act. It can schedule things, send messages, update systems, move files, or trigger workflows. That sounds amazing, and it can be, but mistakes get more expensive when a tool can take action without you noticing. If a copilot drafts the wrong email, you can catch it before it goes out. If an agent sends the wrong email, it might already be done. That's why agents require stronger guardrails—permissions, approvals, logging, and clear rules about when a human must sign off.

Now here's the reality check. A lot of what you hear about "smart partners" is hype. Real systems today work best in narrow lanes with clear rules. They can do routine work fast, but they still struggle with messy human situations, unclear goals, and decisions that involve values and consequences. A tool that moves faster than you do can multiply good work, but it can also multiply chaos. If your process is sloppy, AI doesn't fix it. It automates the sloppiness at high speed.

Is It Safe?

For Analog readers, it's backwards to teach "how to use AI" before answering the question you're already holding: **Is it safe?**

Here's the first truth you need to hear. AI did not create surveillance. You already live inside a surveillance economy. Loyalty cards track what you buy. Phones track where you go. Apps track what you click. Google and Facebook built massive systems around attention and data long before today's AI boom. AI is best understood as an intelligence layer added on top of systems that have been collecting information for years. That context matters because it stops you from treating AI like a brand-new monster. It's not brand-new. It's an upgrade to an existing machine.

So, before you use any AI tool, you need a simple three-question framework. The first question is: **Who owns this platform, and what is their business model?** If the product is free, you are almost certainly the product. That doesn't mean it's evil. It means you should assume they make money from data, ads, or selling services to businesses.

The second question is: **What do they keep, and for how long?** This is where you look for phrases like "may be used to improve our models." When you see language like that, it often means your inputs can be retained and used to train future versions, unless you change settings or opt out. You don't need to memorize legal terms. You just need to recognize the pattern: if they say they can use your data to improve the system, you should treat what you type as something that might be stored and shared.

The third question is: **What are my rights, and how do I use them?** Can you delete your data? Can you opt out of training use? Can you close the account and remove your history? If you can't figure out how to exercise your rights, then functionally, you don't have them. A safe tool is not just about promises. It's about controls you can actually use.

The AI You Didn't Install

Here's something most Analogs don't realize yet. You don't have to sign up for AI to be using it. AI is already inside the software you've been using for years.

If you use Microsoft Word, Outlook or Microsoft Office, you've probably seen Copilot appear in your ribbon. If you use Adobe Acrobat, you've noticed the AI Assistant icon that didn't used to be there. If you use Gmail, you've watched Smart Compose finish your sentences. If you use Windows 11, you may have heard of a feature called Recall that takes periodic snapshots of what's on your screen. None of these features required you to download a new app or create a new account. They arrived through routine software updates, sometimes turned on by default.

This isn't a conspiracy. It's the current default behavior of the software industry. Major vendors are adding AI features to their products and enabling them for most users, and most users never notice. That's a problem because the three-question framework we just walked through doesn't apply automatically to software you didn't consciously choose to start using with AI.

So apply it now, deliberately, to the tools you already have on your devices.

Who owns the platform, and what is their business model? Microsoft, Adobe, and Google all make money from enterprise software subscriptions. That's good news—they don't need to sell your data to survive. But they do use customer data to improve their AI models unless you specifically opt out. The default setting is usually "participate." Your job is to know that and decide whether to change it.

What do they keep, and for how long? When you use Copilot inside Word, your document contents may be sent to Microsoft's servers for processing. When you use Acrobat's AI Assistant, the PDF content you're working on may be transmitted to Adobe. In most cases, these vendors have improved their enterprise-tier privacy protections significantly in recent years, but the consumer-tier defaults are often looser. Check which tier you're actually on.

What are your rights, and how do you use them? Every one of these embedded AI features can be turned off. The settings are not always obvious, but they exist. Microsoft 365 has a Copilot settings page. Adobe Acrobat has an AI preferences section. Gmail has a Smart Features toggle. Windows 11

Recall can be disabled entirely. If you want to take five minutes and audit what's running, you can. Most people never do.

Here's the practical takeaway for personal use. For most Analog readers using these tools for personal email, personal documents, and personal projects, the embedded AI features are generally safe to use if you apply the Four Rules coming up next. You don't need to turn everything off. You need to know it's there, and you need to apply the same discipline you'd apply to any AI tool.

There is one audience where the stakes are different, and that's business owners. If you have customer records, employee information, financial documents, or regulated data on your devices, the embedded AI conversation requires more than a brief sidebar in this book. For that audience, I've put together a free companion resource that walks through the specific settings, the specific audit steps, and the specific policy language small business owners need. You'll find the Data Hygiene Checklist link on the last page of the book. If that's not you, keep reading—the Four Rules below will serve you well.

Four Rules

Now for the operational baseline: four rules that work for almost every AI interaction—whether you're using a standalone AI tool or the embedded AI features we just discussed. These are non-negotiable if you want to use AI without regret. Rule one is **anonymize before you paste**. Remove names, account numbers, addresses, diagnosis codes, student IDs, anything that ties the content to a real person or a real account. If you wouldn't put it on a public whiteboard, don't paste it in as-is.

Rule two is **summarize rather than reproduce**. Describe the document instead of pasting the whole document. You can say, "Here's what this contract says," or "Here are the key points in this report," and ask for help organizing or drafting a response. You get most of the benefit without handing over the full raw material.

Rule three is the most important single fact for this audience to understand: **consumer AI is not HIPAA-covered.** That means medical data you submit to a general consumer chatbot is not protected by federal health privacy law the way it would be inside a hospital system or a covered healthcare platform. ***If you remember only one safety point in this book, remember that one.***

Rule four is simple: **treat AI conversations like a postcard, not a sealed letter.** A sealed letter is private. A postcard can be read. You don't need to panic about that, but you do need to behave like an adult. Assume it could be seen. Act accordingly.

These rules are not a reason to avoid AI. They are the reason you can use it with confidence. Most people using AI every day have never thought this through. They paste private information, trust the tool blindly, and hope nothing goes wrong. You're going to do better than that because you developed key skills as an Analog. Once you understand where a tool sits on the AI spectrum, and once you apply the three questions and the four rules, you stop being a passive user and become a controlled operator.

PART II

The Analog Advantage: Why Your Generation Has Hidden Strength

Chapter 5 – You're Not Behind – You're Unseduced

If you were watching TV in the 1970s or 1980s, you may have seen a little show called **Columbo**. It didn't look like the flashy detective shows you see today. There weren't high-tech labs or dramatic chase scenes every five minutes. Most of the time, you already knew who did it. The real question was how he would prove it.

The detective never looked impressive. He shuffled in wearing a wrinkled raincoat, hair a mess, acting like he'd misplaced his notebook somewhere between the car and the door. He'd be polite. Almost too polite. He'd let the suspect talk. And the suspect was usually the kind of person who looked like they had everything under control—smooth voice, confident smile, perfect story. The suspect's biggest weapon was performance. They sounded smart. They sounded certain. They sounded like the kind of person you weren't supposed to question.

But Columbo didn't get hypnotized by confidence. He listened for the *one* thing that didn't fit. A timeline that was too clean. A detail that was oddly specific. A sentence that slid past the truth without touching it. He'd nod, thank them, and start to leave. Then he'd stop at the door, turn slightly, and say the line everyone remembers: **"Just one more thing..."** And the room would change. Because that one question wasn't random. It was the loose thread. And once you pull the loose thread, the whole sweater falls apart.

That's what most Analogs don't realize about themselves. You have that detective instinct. You've watched confident people be wrong. You've seen polished presentations collapse when reality showed up. You've lived through enough hype cycles, scams, and "guaranteed wins" to know the difference between **sounds right** and **is right**. You don't get as easily seduced by smooth language, shiny packaging, or perfect certainty.

And that matters more now than it ever did before. AI can produce answers that sound confident and professional in seconds. It can create "polished truth-shaped sentences" even when the foundation is weak. In the AI era, the people who struggle most are the ones who think confidence equals correctness. The people who do best are the ones who pause and ask, "Wait… does that actually make sense?" That's smart. That's you.

So, if you feel "behind" because you didn't grow up with this technology, don't buy that story. Your advantage isn't speed. Your advantage is discernment. In a world where the output is easy, the rare skill is noticing what doesn't fit—then asking the one question that forces reality back into the room. That means you're harder to fool, and that is a serious advantage in the AI era. A lot of people see a smooth answer on a screen and assume it must be true. They confuse confidence with accuracy. They confuse speed with wisdom. If you don't fall for that, you're not "late." You're protected.

Superpower – Situational Awareness

If you're an Analog, you've spent decades building something most people don't even realize they're missing: **situational awareness**. That's my plain-English name for signal-to-noise ratio. It's the ability to look at a situation and quickly sense what matters, what doesn't, what's missing, and what's about to go wrong. It's not a mood. It's not a vibe. It's a real cognitive architecture that forms through lived experience—through wins, losses, and lessons you paid for. When you have it, you don't just process information. You prioritize it.

That matters because AI is an output machine. It can generate ten options in seconds. It can write a report that looks professional. It can summarize a meeting and draft an email. But AI does not truly "see" the situation the way a human with situational awareness does. It doesn't feel the hidden risk behind a polite sentence. It doesn't recognize the politics in the room. It doesn't understand which detail will cause a real-world failure later. It predicts language. It does not carry the weight of consequence.

This is why skepticism becomes a strategic asset. Some people treat skepticism like negativity, but that's shallow. Real skepticism is not refusal. It's inspection. It's the habit of asking, "How do we know?" and "What would prove this wrong?" AI needs people like that. AI needs humans who won't believe everything it says just because it says it nicely. If you are the person who asks for evidence, checks the source, and tests the logic, you are not slowing the team down. You are keeping the team from building a decision on polished nonsense.

Common sense matters more now than it did before AI arrived. Before AI, there was a natural limit on how much nonsense could be produced, because nonsense still took time. A five-page memo usually meant somebody put in effort. Now AI can produce five pages in thirty seconds, and it can sound official while being wrong. When words become cheap, judgement becomes expensive. Common sense is what tells you when an answer doesn't fit reality. It's what tells you when the "smart" suggestion is actually unsafe, untested, or missing key context.

HAL 9000 and Skynet Still Lost

If you want a pop-culture picture, think about HAL 9000 and the T-800 with Skynet. In those stories, the machines look undeniable. They look unstoppable. They look smarter, faster, and colder than any person. But humans still prevailed—not because humans were stronger than machines, but because humans could adapt, improvise, and make meaning under pressure. Humans could read the room. Humans could change the plan when the plan broke. That's situational awareness in action. Adapt. Overcome.

You can see that same skill in real life with first responders and service members. Police officers, firefighters, EMTs, and military teams train situational awareness because their work is full of moving parts, incomplete information, and real consequences. They learn to scan for threat signals, notice what doesn't fit, and make fast decisions when the environment is loud, chaotic, and dangerous. It's not "gut feeling." It's practiced attention, built through training and experience, and it helps them stay alive while protecting others. To every police officer, firefighter, EMT, and member of the military reading this: thank you for your service.

So, if you feel slower with the tools, don't panic. Tool speed is learnable. Situational awareness is harder to fake. It's built over time, and it gives you leverage over both people and AI. The AI can generate output, but you can judge reality. The AI can suggest a route, but you can notice when the road ahead is washed out.

You're not behind. You're unseduced. And in an age of confident machines, the unseduced are the ones who keep everyone else from driving straight into the dark. Now let's lean into your talents.

Chapter 6 — The Death of the Idea-Only Era (and What Replaces It)

The air inside Cobo Hall in 1977 smelled like new carpet, cigarette smoke, and fresh paint. The Detroit Auto Show wasn't just a car event back then. It was a hometown parade. You could feel it in the way people stood a little taller when they saw the badges: **GM. Ford. Chrysler.** This was Motor City territory. This was where the future was supposed to be born.

The lights were bright and the music was loud. Cameras flashed. Crowds gathered three rows deep around rotating platforms where the "next big thing" sat under spotlights like royalty. Detroit loved concepts. Every year, the Big Three rolled out cars that stopped traffic—sleek, aerodynamic shells, interiors that looked like space stations, dashboards full of glowing buttons, and "revolutionary" power ideas that sounded like science fiction. The press ate it up. The headlines wrote themselves: *Tomorrow's Car, Today.* People clapped like they were watching history happen.

But outside the show floor, America was still dealing with the aftershocks of the oil crisis. Gas prices and fuel worries had changed what buyers cared about. People still wanted style, sure—but they also wanted something that started every morning, didn't guzzle fuel, and didn't live at the repair shop. That's where the story quietly shifted.

While Detroit was showing visions, Japan was shipping reality.

Toyota and other Japanese automakers weren't winning crowds with futuristic dashboards. They were winning drivers with cars that worked. They built vehicles that were dependable, affordable, and consistent. The promise wasn't "look at this wild idea." The promise was "this will get you to work—again and again." They weren't trying to impress you for five minutes under a spotlight. They were trying to earn your trust for five years on the road.

Detroit was full of idea people. Japan was full of builders.

That difference sounds small until you see the outcome. Concept cars made people dream, but dreams don't carry you 50 miles a day in winter. By the time Detroit fully understood what was happening, foreign automakers had already captured loyalty, market share, and momentum. And momentum is hard to stop once it gets rolling. Toyota didn't just sell cars. It sold confidence—one reliable mile at a time. Later, models like the Camry would become famous for running for hundreds of thousands of miles, not because they were flashy, but because they were built to last.

This is the warning bell for the AI era, and it matters for Analogs. We are leaving an age where **having ideas** made you valuable. We are entering an age where ideas are cheap, because AI can generate them all day. The new advantage is execution—building, testing, delivering, and owning results. Detroit didn't lose because it lacked creativity. It lost because it mistook applause for progress.

Ideas Without Timely Execution Equals Zero

For a long time, ideas felt rare. If you had good ideas and you could explain them well, you could stand out. In many workplaces, the "idea person" became important because they could see what others didn't see. Sometimes they didn't even have to build the thing. They just had to talk about it clearly and sound confident.

That era is ending. Not because ideas don't matter, but because ideas are now cheap.

AI has made idea generation easy for everyone. A person can type one prompt and get ten business ideas, ten marketing angles, or a full "strategy" in minutes. The barrier to producing smart-sounding concepts has dropped fast. So, if your main value was being the one with the ideas, you may feel the ground shifting under your feet.

This is the death of the idea-only era. It can feel harsh, but it is also good news, because what replaces it is more honest.

AI rewards people who can move from idea to action. When AI can generate endless options, the real value becomes choosing the right option and building it. In the AI era, execution becomes the new status. Building becomes the proof.

AI can write a beautiful plan, but it cannot make the plan real. It cannot create trust. It cannot solve human resistance. It cannot handle the messy parts when things go wrong. AI can generate words and steps, but it cannot carry the weight of consequences. That part still belongs to humans.

This is why doers and builders win. They take output and turn it into action. They test ideas in small ways instead of arguing about them for weeks. They gather feedback, fix what's broken, and ship again. AI makes it faster to draft and plan, but it also creates a new problem: too many choices. When you have twenty options, you need someone who can decide. Clear decision-making is becoming one of the most valuable skills in the workplace.

Leadership is changing too. In the past, a leader could walk into a room, deliver a confident strategy, and many people had no quick way to test the claims. Now people have AI in their pocket. They can fact-check statements, ask for sources, and compare "best practices" in seconds. That means weak strategies will get exposed faster. This doesn't make leadership impossible. It makes leadership more real.

And here's where things get uncomfortable for certain leaders. Weak or toxic leaders used to survive because it took a long time for people to gather enough lived experience to name the problem. New hires would arrive hopeful, then slowly notice patterns: unclear priorities, blame-shifting, favoritism, fear-based management, constant emergencies, high turnover, and the same "fire drills" every month. It often took months—or years—before someone could say, with confidence, "This place is broken," or "This leader is the problem."

AI shortens that timeline.

Workers will be able to evaluate leadership and culture faster than ever, because they will have tools to organize signals that used to be scattered. That doesn't mean AI will always be fair or accurate, and it does not mean you should trust gossip. But it does mean this: the information environment is changing, and leaders can't hide behind fog the way they used to.

Imagine what happens when every job posting becomes the start of an investigation. Interested applicants can scan public documents, press releases, leadership interviews, employee reviews, and social media posts to look for patterns. They can compare what a company claims to value with what it actually rewards. They can spot gaps between "we care about people" and "our turnover is constant." They can see whether leaders speak with clarity or hide behind buzzwords. They can look for how leaders respond under pressure—do they take responsibility, or do they blame others?

This used to be hard because it required time and effort. People had to hunt for information, read it all, and connect the dots. Now AI can help people sift through large amounts of public information quickly and summarize the signals. It can highlight repeated themes, contradictions, and warning signs. It can help applicants build better questions for interviews, instead of walking in blind.

That means toxic leadership will be challenged in new ways. A leader who survives by intimidation may still get obedience, but they will struggle to keep talent. A leader who survives by vague vision and constant speeches will be questioned by people who can quickly compare promises to evidence. A leader who hoards knowledge to keep power will face teams that can find information faster and see around bottlenecks. In the AI era, "trust me" becomes a weaker strategy, because people can ask, "Based on what?"

This also means good leaders will stand out faster. Leaders who communicate clearly, make consistent decisions, and treat people with respect will attract stronger applicants. Healthy organizations will benefit because the best workers won't have to guess as much. They will be able to choose better on purpose.

There is one more shift happening at the same time: knowledge hoarding will no longer support identity. For years, some people stayed valuable by controlling information. They became the gate. They knew where the documents were, how the process worked, and what the "real rules" were. AI and modern search tools weaken that kind of power. When information is easier to find, the hoarder loses leverage.

This does not mean expertise is worthless. It means the old kind of power— "I know something you don't"—is fading. True expertise is not hiding information. True expertise is judgement. It's knowing what matters, what is missing, what is risky, and what will happen next. AI doesn't remove the need for that. It increases it, because there is more noise than ever.

Some readers hear all of this and think, "So I need to become a programmer." Most people do not. Reinvention in the AI era is not about learning to code. It is about learning how to use AI as a tool while keeping your identity and your responsibility. It means you learn how to delegate the easy parts to AI—drafting, organizing, summarizing—while you keep the human parts: judgement, ethics, context, and decisions.

If you are an Analog, you don't have to surrender who you are. You do need to upgrade how you operate. Your value can shift from "I'm the person with the answers" to "I'm the person who can find the truth, make the call, and build the result." In a world where ideas are easy, that ability becomes rare.

What replaces the idea-only era is an era of proof. Not perfect proof. Not "never make mistakes" proof. Real proof, like prototypes, pilots, small tests, feedback loops, and measurable outcomes. AI makes it easier to move quickly, so the leaders who matter will be the ones who can build fast, learn fast, and still hold the line on ethics and accountability.

Here is the challenge at the end of this chapter. If your identity has been built on being the idea person, keep your ideas—but stop living there. In the AI era, ideas are the beginning, not the finish line. The world won't reward the loudest vision. It will reward the people who can turn vision into something real—and the leaders who can no longer hide behind words.

Chapter 7 — Amplified Intelligence: When Humans and AI Become a Team

April 13, 1970 started like a normal day in space. Routine voice checks. Routine switches. Routine confidence. Apollo 13 was already nearly 200,000 miles from Earth, moving through black silence where "help" was not a phone call away. Up there, small things matter. A single knob. A single valve. A single decision made out of habit.

Then came the stir.

An astronaut flipped the switch to stir the oxygen tanks—something they'd done before, something that was supposed to keep the system stable. A quiet action. A normal procedure. And then, without warning, the spacecraft shuddered. A sharp bang. A jolt that felt wrong in a place where everything is measured and controlled. The lights flickered. Warning alarms screamed. Instruments jumped. For a moment, the cabin filled with the kind of silence that isn't calm. It's shock.

"Houston, we've had a problem."

On Earth, a problem means inconvenience. In space, a problem can become a countdown.

An oxygen tank had exploded, ripping open the life support system like a puncture in a lung. Oxygen wasn't just for breathing. It fed the fuel cells that made electricity. Losing oxygen meant losing power. Losing power meant losing heat, navigation, and systems that kept the crew alive. The spacecraft was still flying, but it had been wounded—badly—and it was far from home.

The onboard computer could do math, but it couldn't solve the crisis. It could manage trajectory, but it couldn't invent a new plan out of thin air. The astronauts could troubleshoot, but they couldn't see the entire system the way a room full of engineers could. They were also fighting cold, fatigue, and the slow panic that creeps in when you realize the rules you trained for no longer apply.

Back in Houston, Mission Control became a furnace of focused brains. Rows of engineers leaned over consoles and legal pads. Slide rules came out. Checklists were torn open, rewritten, crossed out, rewritten again. Nobody was performing. Nobody was trying to sound smart. They were trying to keep three men alive.

And here's the part people forget: this wasn't just a technical problem. It was a resource problem. You can't order parts in space. You can't run to the store. Whatever you have is whatever you have. So, Houston did something that sounds simple and is actually genius: they built a solution using only the parts already on the spacecraft. They took the manifest—the list of what was onboard—and treated it like a survival menu.

Carbon dioxide was rising because the astronauts had moved into the lunar module to use it as a lifeboat. The filters didn't match. The square filters from one module didn't fit the round openings of the other. In normal life, you'd buy an adapter. In space, you make one. Mission Control created a plan to build a carbon dioxide filter out of whatever was available—plastic, cardboard, hoses, and the most famous piece of equipment in American problem-solving history: duct tape.

The astronauts didn't just "figure it out." They followed instructions from humans on the ground who were building the fix at the same time, step by step, with the same parts, in a room full of pressure and sweat. The crew assembled it in the cold cabin. The levels stabilized. The air became breathable again.

And while that was happening, the computer did what it does best. It handled calculations and supported the flight path back toward Earth. It helped manage the trajectory. It helped the ship obey physics. But it didn't decide what mattered. It didn't feel the stakes. It didn't invent meaning. It didn't lead.

Humans did.

Apollo 13 wasn't a story about humans winning alone. It wasn't a story about technology saving the day by itself. It was a human-plus-machine story where neither half could have done it alone. The computer managed the trajectory. The humans managed the meaning. They turned panic into process. They turned a broken system into a survivable one. And they brought three men home from the void.

Human and AI Collaboration

For most of human history, the problem was getting information. Now the problem is surviving it. In the last few decades, we built systems that create data all day and all night. Emails, dashboards, tickets, reports, alerts, news, meetings, and messages keep coming whether you are ready or not. In almost every profession, the amount of useful information now exceeds what any one person can read and process in real time. That is true no matter how smart you are and no matter how hard you work.

So, if you have felt behind, overloaded, or tired, hear this clearly: **the method broke. You did not.** The old method was simple—read everything, keep up, remember it all, and respond fast. That worked when the stream was small. Now the stream is a flood. This is not a personal failure of attention or discipline. It is a structural problem caused by the volume and speed of modern work.

This is where AI can become a real partner. Not by thinking for you, and not by replacing your judgement, but by sifting through information at a scale no human can match. AI can scan, sort, summarize, compare, and group large amounts of text and data. It can pull out patterns, themes, and changes. It can take a pile of messy notes and turn it into a clean outline. It can return what matters most—**but only if you define what "matters" means.** AI is a sieve. You decide what you're trying to catch.

Now comes the real test: can you build what only the awakened can see? This is the threshold where vision either becomes real structure—or dies as a nice idea. The leaders of the next era won't be defined only by titles or years in the job. They will be defined by their ability to build, collaborate, and integrate across both human thinking and machine capability. This is where a new kind of value shows up.

Welcome to the domain of the **Amplified Contributor**. This is not a job title or a department. It is a new kind of value-creation. It is a way of thinking and building that fuses human insight with machine power on purpose. In older systems, contribution was measured by time, effort, and visibility. In amplified systems, contribution is measured by how well you see patterns, how fast you co-create, and how well you direct the flow of intelligence across both humans and AI tools.

That does not mean everyone needs to become a programmer. It means everyone needs a new core skill: knowing what to delegate to AI and what to keep in human hands. Delegate work that is heavy, repetitive, and pattern-based. Let AI do first drafts, summaries, comparisons, lists of options, and organization. Use it to reduce the time you spend drowning in raw material. Then keep the work that requires judgement, values, and consequences. Keep the final decisions. Keep the parts where being wrong hurts people, breaks trust, creates legal risk, or damages relationships. A simple rule helps: let AI do the first 80%, but you do the last 20%. That last 20% is where reality lives.

To stay safe and effective, you must remain the driver, not the passenger. AI can sound confident even when it is wrong. It can produce writing that looks professional while hiding weak assumptions. So, you must set the goal, not the tool. You must define the audience, the purpose, the constraints, and what a "good" answer looks like. You must also verify the load-bearing facts—names, dates, numbers, quotes, and any claim that could cause damage if wrong. Don't treat AI like a boss. Treat it like a fast assistant that needs supervision.

This leads to the most important agreement in the chapter: the **Human-in-the-Loop contract**. It is simple and non-negotiable. **You own the outcome, regardless of who—or what—did the work.** If an AI draft goes out with an error, you own it. If an AI summary misses the key point, you own it. If an AI-powered plan causes harm, the tool won't take responsibility. Your name and your organization will. "Human in the loop" means AI can help with speed and structure, but a human must check the work where it matters and signs off only when they are ready to stand behind it.

Now we get to the deeper level: what separates people who "use AI" from people who actually reshape value with it. The Amplified Contributor develops five converged domains. These are not soft skills. They are survival skills for the next era. If you ignore them, you become a bottleneck. If you build them, you become hard to replace—not because you know more facts, but because you synthesize, act, and adapt better.

The first domain is **Cognitive Mastery**. The future belongs to people who can make sense faster without becoming reactive. That means you can shift mental models when reality changes. It means you can hold more than one truth long enough to find the deeper pattern. It means you keep systemic awareness even under pressure. In a world with endless information, wisdom is the filter, and clarity is the superpower. And you've had decades to develop this versus the Digitals generation.

The second domain is **AI Fluency**. You don't need to be a prompt engineer. You need to be a prompt strategist. You learn how to ask better questions, how to give better context, and how to shape the output so it is actually useful. You can use AI to test scenarios, explore options, and reflect on blind spots. You stay human in the loop by shaping tone, ethics, and action. This isn't technical magic. It's cognitive jiu-jitsu—designing the conversation so it drives insight instead of noise.

The third domain is **Psychological Resilience**. In the AI era, you will be wrong more often, and sometimes more publicly, because things move faster. The question is whether you can adapt without collapsing into ego or shame. Amplified contributors detach identity from being right. They find meaning inside change. They rewrite their own internal stories as fast as the systems evolve around them. The new leadership trait isn't certainty. It's identity agility.

The fourth domain is **Human Collaboration and Narrative**. The future isn't human versus machine. It's human plus machine plus many other humans, working together in shifting teams. That requires the ability to create coherence across roles, departments, and tools. It requires story—because story is how humans align emotion, purpose, and execution. Storytelling is not decoration. It is operational connective tissue. It builds trust, focus, and shared direction.

The fifth domain is **Builder Mindset**. Insight isn't enough. You have to ship. You prototype in days, not quarters. You improve through feedback, not ego. You own outcomes even when the process is shared with AI tools. This is about living in learning loops instead of waiting for perfection.

Put it all together and you get the real promise of amplified intelligence. AI is not here to replace your mind. It is here to solve the structural problem of overload by sifting at scale. You remain responsible for meaning, ethics, and decisions. When you learn to delegate wisely, stay the driver, and honor the human-in-the-loop contract, you don't become less human. You become amplified—and you become the kind of contributor the next era is built around. Welcome to the party, pal.

PART III

Your First 30 Days with AI (No Tech Background Required)

Chapter 8 — Setup Without the Headache

My dad left the VCR clock blinking **12:00** for so long it stopped looking like a mistake and started looking like a choice. Every time I walked into the living room, that green flashing number stared back like a tiny flag that said, "Nope."

I'd point at it and say, "Dad, you know that's nct the time, right?" He'd shrug.

"Doesn't matter," he'd say. "If I want to record something, I can just hit record."

And he could—kind of. He could record "MacGyver" the manual way, but only if he was sitting there when it started. If dinner ran late or the phone rang, he'd miss the first ten minutes and pretend it didn't matter. The timer-record setup was a seven-step maze: set the clock, program the channel, start time, end time, AM or PM, input source, confirm it all in the exact order the machine demanded. My dad could fix plenty of real-world problems, but the VCR was pure friction.

The funny part was that my dad wasn't a confused man. He could rebuild an engine. He could argue with a contractor and win. He could navigate a city with nothing but landmarks and instinct. But the VCR timer? That thing was a seven-step puzzle box designed by someone who hated humans. Set the clock. Find the program button. Pick the channel. Choose the start time. Choose the end time. Make sure it's AM and not PM. Confirm it's not recording the wrong input. Then hit "Enter" in the exact way the VCR demanded, not the way a normal person would.

For fifteen years, the blinking 12:00 on the VCR was the universal symbol of technology anxiety. You could record "MacGyver" manually. But the seven-step timer-record process defeated an entire generation of otherwise highly capable adults. The VCR didn't become useless because people couldn't figure out the clock. It became the most powerful entertainment shift of the decade. People found workarounds. They recorded what they could. They got value anyway.

One day I finally set it for him. The blinking stopped. The display went calm. Dad stared at it, nodded once, and said, "Okay. Now don't touch it."

That's the point: friction can make smart people avoid good tools. But AI setup is not the VCR clock. These tools are built for quick, low-friction entry. The hard doorway is an illusion. This chapter is proof.

So don't leave AI blinking 12:00 in your life and tell yourself you'll "just hit record when you need to." Step through the doorway once, and you unlock the real value.

Less Friction Than The VCR

Most people don't avoid AI because they hate technology. They avoid it because setup feels like a trap. New accounts, new passwords, new apps, new terms you don't want to read, and the fear that one wrong click will leak something private. This chapter is here to make your first steps simple, safe, and low-stress.

The first decision is picking a tool. For beginners, the most important thing is not the "best model." It's whether the tool is easy to use, works on the device you already have, and has privacy controls you understand. Free tools are fine for learning. Paid tools usually give you higher limits, faster responses, and sometimes better privacy options for work settings, but you don't need to pay on day one unless you're using it daily or you keep hitting limits. If you're choosing a tool for work, look for business or workplace versions that clearly say your data isn't used to train models by default. (Some services spell this out directly for business tiers.)

Privacy matters even when you're "just trying it." Here's the beginner rule that keeps you safe: don't feed the tool anything you'd regret seeing on a billboard. Consumer AI tools can store conversations, and some may use your inputs to improve their systems unless you change settings or opt out. That's why it's worth taking two minutes to find the privacy settings and look for options like "don't use my content for training" or "opt out of model improvement." (Different platforms use different words, but the idea is the same.)

Now decide free vs. paid with one simple question: how often will you use this? If you're experimenting a few times a week, free is usually enough. If you're using it every day for writing, planning, summarizing, or school/work tasks, a paid tier can reduce frustration because you'll hit fewer caps and wait less. If you're using AI around sensitive work topics, consider a business/work plan through your organization, because those often come with stronger controls and clearer privacy promises.

Next comes accounts and logins. Keep this boring on purpose. Use a real email you can access easily, and choose a strong password you won't forget. If the tool offers two-factor authentication (2FA), turn it on. It's one extra step at login, but it prevents a lot of headaches later. Also, avoid signing up through random links. Go through the official site or app store so you don't land on a fake copy.

Now let's talk devices, because this is where beginners get stuck. If you want the easiest starting point, start on the device you're most comfortable reading and typing on. For most people, that is either a phone or a laptop.

A phone is the simplest way to begin because it's always with you and setup is quick. It's great for short questions, quick summaries, and "help me write a text/email" moments. The downside is that a phone can make you sloppy. Small screens encourage copy-paste mistakes, and people are more likely to paste private details without thinking. If you start on a phone, treat it like a notepad for low-risk use until your habits are solid.

A laptop (or desktop) is the best choice if you plan to do real work with AI. The bigger screen helps you read carefully, compare drafts, and check details before you send anything. It's also easier to manage files, organize notes, and copy text without losing context. If you're learning for professional use, start on a laptop whenever possible.

A tablet sits in the middle. It's comfortable for reading, reviewing, and editing, and it can be great with a keyboard. But if you don't already use a tablet for work, you don't need to buy one just for AI. Start with what you already have.

Here's a simple setup path that works for almost everyone. First, choose one tool and use only that tool for two weeks so you don't confuse yourself. Second, create your account, turn on 2FA, and find the privacy settings. Third, write your first three prompts in "safe mode": ask for help drafting something general, summarizing something non-private, or creating a checklist. Build confidence before you bring it into anything sensitive.

Finally, remember the point of setup. You are not trying to "become an AI person." You're building a stable on-ramp. Once the tool is installed, the account is secured, and your privacy habits are in place, the rest of the book gets easier—because you'll stop fighting the doorway and start learning the skill.

Now let's get into two setups examples to demystify the process.

OpenAI's ChatGPT

ChatGPT is popular because it is simple. You don't need special software skills to start. You type a question like you would ask a person, and it answers back in plain language. That ease of use is a big reason why so many people are trying it. It feels less like "learning a new computer program" and more like having a helpful assistant on call. OpenAI says ChatGPT is used by hundreds of millions of people for learning, work, and everyday decisions, which tells you it has already gone mainstream.

Before you sign up, you only need a few basics. You need a working email address that you can open right away, because you may need to verify your account. Gmail, Outlook, and Yahoo are common choices because they tend to work smoothly with verification emails. You also need to meet the age requirement. OpenAI says ChatGPT is not meant for children under 13, and ages 13 to 18 should have parental consent.

Prerequisites

- Valid email address (Gmail, Outlook, or Yahoo recommended)
- Must be 13+ (18+ without parental consent in most regions)
- Available in supported countries

To create an account, you go to ChatGPT in a web browser at chatgpt.com, or you can use the official mobile apps on iOS or Android. Once you're there, you select **Sign Up**. You will usually have a few choices: you can create an account with an email address, or you can use a sign-in option like Google, Apple, or Microsoft. The easiest path for most beginners is to pick the method you already use and trust, because it reduces password chaos.

If you use email sign-up, you create a password and then verify your email through a link sent to your inbox. After that, the system may ask for basic profile details like your name and date of birth. Some setups also include phone verification by SMS to confirm you're a real person and to reduce abuse. Then you accept OpenAI's terms and usage policies and you're in.

Account Creation

1. Navigate to chatgpt.com in a web browser (or download the desktop app for Mac/Windows, or mobile app for iOS/Android)
2. Click "Sign Up for Free" – options include email, Google, Microsoft, or Apple account
3. If using email, create a password and verify via link sent to your inbox
4. Enter your name and date of birth
5. Verify your phone number via SMS
6. Accept OpenAI's terms of service and usage policies

Post-Setup

After setup, the free tier is a real starting point. It is designed for everyday use, but it has limits during busy periods and for higher-capability models. OpenAI explains that free tier access to the most capable models is limited within a five-hour window, and you'll be notified if you hit the limit and offered an upgrade.

One more reality check: OpenAI began testing ads for Free (and Go) users in the U.S. starting

February 9, 2026. Ads are meant to support free access, and OpenAI states that ads are clearly labeled and do not influence answers. If you upgrade to a paid plan, ads are removed.

Once you're logged in, there are a couple optional settings that can make your experience better. One is **Custom Instructions**, where you can tell ChatGPT how you like responses written (short, step-by-step, friendly, formal) and give it basic preferences that carry across chats. You can also change appearance settings like theme. OpenAI also notes that creating custom GPTs is available on paid plans rather than Free.

Anthropic's Claude

Claude is popular for the same reason ChatGPT is popular: it feels simple. You open a site, type like you're talking to a person, and you get a clear answer back. For beginners, that "no complicated menus" feeling matters. You don't have to be technical to get value on day one—you just need a basic setup that works.

Before you sign up, there are a few prerequisites. You need to be in a supported location, because

Claude is not available everywhere. Anthropic keeps a public list of supported countries and regions, and access depends on where you are. You also need to meet the age requirement. Anthropic states you must be at least 18 years old to use Claude.

Account setup is straightforward. You can use Claude in a web browser at **claude.ai**, or you can use the official desktop app for Mac/Windows, or the mobile apps on iOS/Android. When you arrive, Claude gives you two common login paths: "Continue with Google" or "Continue with email." If you choose Google, you sign in with your Google account the way you do on many other sites. If you choose email, Claude sends you a secure login link (sometimes called a "magic link") to your inbox, and clicking it logs you in.

Account Creation

1. Navigate to claude.ai in a web browser (or download the desktop app for Mac/Windows, or mobile app for iOS/Android)
2. Sign up via email or Google account

3. If using email, click the magic link sent to your inbox
4. Verify your phone number and confirm you are at least 18 years old
5. Enter your name
6. Accept the usage policy and terms of service

One detail that helps beginners: because Claude can use an emailed login link, it can reduce password headaches. But it also means you need reliable access to your email account. If you request the login email on one device but click the link on a different device, Claude may give you a verification code you enter back on the original device to finish signing in.

After you're set up, Claude's free plan is a real starting point. Anthropic offers multiple plans (Free, Pro, Max, Team, and Enterprise), and you can start on Free to learn the basics before deciding if you need more capacity. If you do upgrade later, it's usually because you want higher usage limits, priority access during busy times, or additional features that come with paid tiers.

On the "ads" question, Claude is positioned differently from ChatGPT right now. Anthropic has publicly said Claude will remain ad-free, and they've been loud about that choice. That doesn't automatically make Claude "more private," but it does mean you're less likely to deal with ad-related distractions in the product experience.

Finally, once you're logged in, treat personalization as optional—not required. The main win is getting comfortable asking Claude for practical help (summaries, drafts, checklists, explanations). You can explore settings later. For now, the safest beginner approach is the same rule you already know from this book: don't paste sensitive personal or work data into any consumer AI tool unless you're sure about the data controls and retention rules for that specific plan and use case.

Setup steps and plan options will keep changing. That's normal in a fast-moving tech world. Companies update features, rename buttons, and change what is free or paid. If you try to memorize every screen, you'll stay frustrated. Instead, focus on the core steps that don't change: choose a trusted tool, protect your privacy, secure your account, and start with low-risk practice until you feel comfortable.

That's why this chapter focuses on what stays the same. If you can answer three questions—who owns the tool, what data it keeps, and what control you have—you can handle most changes without stress.

If you want the most up-to-date walkthroughs with screenshots and video demos, I keep them free on my website: AIForAnalogs.com.

I understand tech setups can be frustrating. That's normal, and it doesn't mean you're doing anything wrong. The important part is this: now that we've gotten through setup, the hard doorway is behind you.

In the next chapter, we'll show you "super prompts" you can use right away, so you sound like a pro out of the gates—even if you're brand new to AI.

Chapter 9: Prompting for Analogs — The 5-Part Formula

In the late 1970s and 1980s, a lot of executives didn't "write" the way we think of writing today. They dictated. Some spoke into a Dictaphone. Some stood in a doorway with a coffee in hand and spoke fast while a secretary took notes. And every one of them learned the same lesson the hard way.

An executive would come back from a meeting, drop into a chair, and say something like, "Write a memo about the meeting." Then they'd go back to their day and assume the job was done. A few hours later, the memo would land on their desk. It wasn't wrong. It just wasn't *right*. It captured what the secretary thought was important. It missed the one decision the executive cared about. It sounded too soft when it needed authority, or too harsh when it needed trust. The executive would sigh, mark it up, and mutter, "That's not what I meant."

But the secretary wasn't the problem. The instruction was.

The executives who got great results were the ones who learned to speak in specifics. They'd say, "Write a two-page memo summarizing the three decisions we made this morning. Address it to the regional managers. Keep the tone firm but supportive. List action items under each decision. Add a follow-up deadline for next Friday. Close with a short paragraph explaining why this matters." And when that memo came back, it wasn't a guess. It was a mirror of what they asked for. Clear input produced clear output.

That's exactly how AI works.

AI prompting is dictation to the most capable assistant you've ever had. It can draft faster than any human. It can reorganize your thoughts in seconds. It can write in almost any tone you want. But it still needs direction. If you give it a vague request, it will fill in the blanks with its best guess. If you give it a clear request, it will give you work that feels like it read your mind—because you finally told it what your mind actually wanted.

So, when you learn prompting, you're not learning "tech." You're learning communication. You're learning how to give the kind of instructions that produce results you can use right away. The secretary wasn't the problem. The prompt was. And in the AI era, that same truth can turn frustration into leverage in about ten minutes.

What is Prompting?

Artificial intelligence is powerful, but it is not magic. It responds to direction. The quality of what it produces depends on how clearly a person explains the task and the goal. This is where prompting comes in.

In simple terms, prompting is the act of telling an AI what you want it to do. Prompt engineering is the more careful version of that process. It means shaping your request so the AI can give a useful powerful answer. When a prompt is vague, the result is usually vague. When a prompt is clear, the result is usually clearer and more helpful.

Think of it like giving instructions to a capable assistant. If you simply say, "Help me with this," the assistant has to guess what you mean. If you explain the goal, the situation, and the type of result you want, the assistant can work much more effectively. AI works in a similar way. The better your instructions, the better the outcome.

This is important because AI is becoming a common tool in work, research, education, and everyday life. People now use AI to write drafts, organize ideas, analyze problems, and plan projects. When someone learns how to prompt well, the tool becomes far more useful. It helps people think faster, organize ideas more clearly, and explore options they might not have considered on their own.

Understanding prompting changes how people use AI. At first, many people treat AI like a search engine. They ask it questions and read the answers. That can be helpful, but it only uses a small part of what the technology can do. When people learn how to communicate with AI more clearly, the tool becomes more like a partner. It can help analyze problems, refine ideas, draft plans, and support decision making.

Poor prompts don't "break" AI, but they do push it into its weakest mode: guessing. When you give a vague prompt like "Tell me about this" or "Write a plan," the AI has to fill in missing details. It doesn't know your situation, your audience, your goals, or your limits unless you tell it. So, it starts making reasonable-sounding assumptions. The more blanks you leave, the more it has to invent to produce a complete answer.

That invention is where hallucinations show up. An AI hallucination is when the tool gives you an answer that sounds confident and polished but is not true or not supported by real evidence. It might make up a statistic, a quote, a policy, a law, a book title, or a source that does not exist. It may also mix up names, dates, and details in a way that feels believable. The scary part is that it can do this calmly, with professional language, which makes people trust it more than they should.

Hallucinations happen because most AI tools are built to keep responding, even when the information is unclear. They are prediction engines. They predict what a good answer should sound like based on patterns they learned. If your prompt is missing key facts, the AI can still produce an answer that fits the pattern of an answer—even if it isn't anchored to reality. It's like a coworker who hates saying "I don't know," so they guess instead, but they guess with great grammar.

Poor prompts make this worse in three common ways. First, vague prompts don't give the AI enough context, so it fills the gaps with assumptions. Second, prompts that ask for facts without asking for sources invite the AI to produce "fact-shaped" sentences without proving anything. Third, prompts that demand a confident tone ("give me the best answer") can encourage the AI to sound certain even when the situation is uncertain.

Good prompts reduce hallucinations by forcing clarity. When you give a role, a clear objective, real context, and constraints, the AI has fewer reasons to guess. When you ask for sources, and when you tell it to flag uncertainty, you push it toward honesty instead of smoothness. And when you verify the load-bearing parts—names, numbers, quotes, dates—you catch the few mistakes that still slip through.

The simple takeaway is this: AI hallucinates more when it has to "perform" without enough information. If you want safer, stronger answers, don't make it perform. Make it work—by giving it a better prompt and checking what matters.

In other words, AI can move from being a simple knowledge translator to becoming a powerful thinking assistant. Knowing how to "speak" to AI allows people to use it to navigate complex problems, organize information, and develop new ideas. In a fast-changing world, this ability becomes a practical advantage.

The 5-Part Formula

To help people do this well, it is useful to follow a simple structure for prompts. One of the most reliable approaches is the **5-Part Formula**. This formula includes five parts: **Role, Goal, Context, Inputs, and Output Format**. Each part helps the AI understand what you need.

The first part is **Role**. This tells the AI who it should act like when answering your request. It sets the perspective for the response. For example, you might ask the AI to act as a writing coach, a strategy advisor, a teacher, or a cybersecurity analyst. When the AI knows the role, it can frame its answer in a more useful way. Saying "Act as a leadership coach" will produce a different answer than simply asking a general question about leadership. The role shapes how the AI thinks about the problem.

The second part is **Goal**. This explains what success looks like. Many people ask AI for something without explaining the result they want to achieve. For example, asking "Write an email" is less helpful than saying "Write an email that reassures the client and asks for a meeting to solve the problem."

The second request tells the AI what the message should accomplish. When the goal is clear, the response is more focused and useful.

The third part is **Context**. Context explains the situation around the task. This might include the audience, the tone, the limits, or the time frame. For example, a message written for executives should sound different than a message written for students. A response that must fit on one page will look different than a long report. Context gives the AI the background information it needs so it does not have to guess.

The fourth part is **Inputs**. Inputs are the materials you give the AI to work with. They are additional information for a better response from the AI. These may include notes, bullet points, draft text, research summaries, or links. When you provide inputs, the AI can organize, summarize, or improve your material. Without inputs, it often produces more general information. Providing clear inputs allows the AI to work directly with your ideas.

The fifth part is **Output Format**. This tells the AI what kind of result you want back. For example, you might ask for a checklist, a short report, an email draft, a table, or a step-by-step plan. Many disappointing AI responses happen simply because the format was not specified. If you tell the AI exactly what type of answer you want, the result is more likely to be useful right away.

When these five parts are combined, the prompt becomes much stronger. Instead of a vague request, it becomes a clear set of instructions. For example, a simple request might say, "Help me think about employee burnout." A stronger prompt would say: "Act as an organizational leadership advisor. Help me explain employee burnout so managers can recognize it early. This is for mid-level managers in a training workshop. Use these themes: workload overload, emotional fatigue, and lack of recognition. Present the answer as a short guide with five action steps."

The second prompt works better because it tells the AI how to think, what to focus on, and what form the answer should take. This reduces confusion and leads to a better result.

Learning to prompt well changes how people work with AI. Instead of simply asking questions, people begin to guide the conversation. They can ask the

AI to analyze options, critique ideas, outline plans, or organize research. This makes the tool far more valuable in real work.

For example, a teacher can use AI to build lesson plans from rough notes. A manager can prepare for a difficult conversation by asking AI to suggest approaches. A researcher can organize complex ideas into a clear outline. A business leader can ask AI to analyze the strengths and risks of a new project. In each case, the value comes from how clearly the prompt is written.

Because of this, prompting is becoming a new form of digital literacy. In the past, digital literacy meant knowing how to search the Internet and use software tools. Today it also means knowing how to communicate effectively with AI. People who learn this skill can use AI to support thinking, planning, writing, and problem solving.

Prompting does not require technical expertise. It requires clarity. When people learn to explain their goals, provide context, and ask for specific formats, the quality of AI responses improves dramatically.

In the end, prompting is about communication. The clearer the communication, the better the collaboration. The **5-Part Formula—Role, Goal, Context, Inputs, and Output Format—** provides a simple and reliable way to guide AI toward useful answers.

As AI becomes more common in everyday work, this skill will matter more and more. Those who know how to communicate with AI effectively will not only find information faster. They will also gain a powerful partner for thinking, planning, and navigating the challenges of a changing world.

The Analog's Super Prompt

A "super prompt" is just a smart way to talk to AI so it stops guessing and starts helping. Most people type a short request like, "Write me an email" or "Give me a plan." The AI will still answer, but it has to fill in the blanks. That's when you get generic results, wrong assumptions, or advice that doesn't fit your situation.

This template works because it gives the AI the same things a good human helper would need: who it should be, what you want, what's going on, what limits matter, what questions must be answered, and what the final output should look like. When you do that, the AI has less room to wander and more room to deliver something useful. The best part is that this format works across almost any AI tool—ChatGPT, Claude, Gemini, Copilot—because all of them respond better when your request is clear and structured.

Here's the key idea: **you are not writing a longer prompt—you are writing a clearer prompt.** You're building a small set of "instructions" that guides the AI like guardrails on a road. That is why the results feel massively more powerful.

The AI Super Prompt Template

Use this exact format. Copy it, paste it, and fill in the blanks.

```
ROLE: Act as a [specific expert type]
advising [who you are / your role].

OBJECTIVE: [One clear sentence stating
exactly what you want the AI to do.]

CONTEXT: [2-4 sentences describing your
situation, what you have, and what
you're working with. The more specific, the
better.]
```

```
CONSTRAINTS: [Any limits — budget, audience,
geography, time, size, tone, etc.]

ANALYSIS REQUIREMENTS:
Provide:
• [Specific thing you want analyzed or
addressed #1]
• [Specific thing #2]
• [Specific thing #3]
• [Add as many as needed]

OUTPUT FORMAT:
Structure the response as a [document type —
report, memo, plan, briefing,
email, etc.] with the following sections:
1. [Section name]
2. [Section name]
3. [Section name]
(Add or remove sections as needed)
```

Why this works so well

ROLE stops the AI from giving you random "Internet average" answers. If you tell it to act like a "career coach," you'll get a different answer than if you tell it to act like an "HR director" or a "small business consultant." You're setting the lens.

OBJECTIVE prevents rambling. One clear sentence tells the AI exactly what "success" looks like.

CONTEXT is where most people fail. The AI cannot see your life. It cannot see your workplace. It cannot see your goals. Context is how you give it the missing pieces so the answer fits *you*, not some imaginary person.

CONSTRAINTS keep it realistic. If you don't say you have a tight budget, it will recommend expensive options. If you don't say your audience is your boss, it may write in the wrong tone. Constraints are the guardrails.

ANALYSIS REQUIREMENTS are your checklist. This is where you tell it what it must cover so it doesn't skip the important parts.

OUTPUT FORMAT makes the result usable right away. If you want a memo, ask for a memo. If you want bullet points, say bullet points. If you want sections, name the sections.

The cheat sheet you can remember

When you're filling this out, ask yourself:

- What kind of expert do I need right now?
- What's the one thing I need done?

- What does the AI need to know about my situation?
- What are my limits and boundaries?
- What specific questions must be answered?
- What should the final answer look like?

Three rules that make the template "super"

Specific beats vague every time. "Mid-size businesses in Michigan" beats "companies." "A 300-word email to my supervisor" beats "write an email."

Tell it who it is. Role assignment is a power move because it shapes the tone, the depth, and the type of advice.

Tell it how to deliver the answer. If you don't control the format, you'll waste time reformatting. If you do control the format, you can copy and use it immediately.

Use this template for almost anything—work decisions, writing, planning, learning, travel, tech choices—and you'll get stronger results because you're turning the AI from a guessing machine into a guided assistant.

Meta Prompting

Most people think prompting is a one-way street. You type a prompt, the AI answers, and you move on. Meta prompting is different. Meta prompting means you use AI to help you get better at prompting. In other words, you don't just ask AI for an answer. You ask AI to teach you how to ask the question in a better way.

This matters because most "bad AI answers" start with a bad prompt. When your request is vague, the AI has to guess. When it guesses, it can invent details, fill gaps with assumptions, or sound confident while being wrong. That is how hallucinations happen. Meta prompting helps you reduce hallucinations by making your prompts clearer before you depend on the output.

The easiest way to meta prompt is to treat the AI like a prompt coach. You can say, "Here is my prompt. Rewrite it using the 5-Part Formula." Or you can say, "Ask me the missing questions you need before you answer." This turns the AI into a guide that helps you add Role, Goal, Context, Inputs, and Output Format—so the tool has fewer blanks to fill.

Meta prompting works best when you do it in two steps. In step one, you ask the AI to improve your prompt, not to answer your question yet. In step two, after you approve the improved prompt, you ask the AI to answer using that better prompt. This small change makes a big difference, because it forces clarity before output.

Here are a few meta prompts you can copy and use. You can paste your rough prompt after them and let the AI clean it up. You are not "cheating." You are using the tool the smart way.

First, you can ask for a rewrite: "Act as a prompt coach. Rewrite my prompt using Role, Objective, Context, Constraints, Analysis Requirements, and Output Format. Then show me the improved prompt and wait for my approval before answering."

Second, you can ask the AI to interview you: "Before you answer, ask me up to five questions to fill in missing context. After I answer, produce the best final response."

Third, you can ask it to stress test your prompt: "Find the assumptions and missing details in my prompt. Tell me what could cause a vague or wrong answer. Then suggest improvements."

Fourth, you can ask it to reduce hallucination risk: "Rewrite my prompt to reduce guessing. Add a request for sources, ask you to flag uncertainty, and tell you to separate facts from assumptions."

The Prompt Super Prompt

Here is an example of a meta prompt to get you started.

```
ROLE: Act as an expert AI prompt engineer
with deep knowledge of how large
language models interpret instructions.

OBJECTIVE: Evaluate the prompt I provide
below and rewrite it as a
significantly more effective version.

CONTEXT: I am a [describe yourself — business
professional, retiree, student,
etc.] trying to use AI to [what you're
generally trying to accomplish].
I wrote the following prompt on my own but
suspect it could produce
better results:

--- MY PROMPT STARTS HERE ---
```

```
[Paste your prompt here exactly as you wrote
it]
--- MY PROMPT ENDS HERE ---

CONSTRAINTS:
- Keep the rewritten prompt understandable —
avoid technical jargon
- Preserve my original intent — improve HOW I
ask, not WHAT I'm asking for
- Assume I will use this with a general-
purpose AI like ChatGPT or Claude

ANALYSIS REQUIREMENTS:
Diagnose my prompt by identifying:
- What is working well
- What is vague, missing, or unclear
- What assumptions the AI might make that
could hurt the result
- What role, context, or constraints I failed
to include

OUTPUT FORMAT:
Structure your response as follows:

1. DIAGNOSIS — What's weak about my current
prompt and why
2. WHAT YOU CHANGED — A plain-English
explanation of every improvement made
3. IMPROVED PROMPT — The fully rewritten,
ready-to-use prompt
4. PRO TIP — One advanced technique I can
apply to future prompts
```

Meta prompting is powerful because it turns AI from a guessing machine into a guided assistant. It also turns you into a better operator over time. After a few weeks, you'll notice you write clearer prompts without even thinking about it. That's the real goal. You don't want one good answer. You want a repeatable method.

The final takeaway is simple. If you want professional-grade results, don't just ask for the output. Ask for a better prompt first. Meta prompting is how you get there fast, and it works across almost any AI product.

If holding all five parts in your head still feels like work, the Analog Twin at AIForAnalogs.com runs the formula for you — you bring the question, it builds the prompt.

Chapter 10 — The Three Lenses Quality Check

Calvin Mercer used to light the town with a ladder and a match. Now he ran a small electrical business with a simple promise: safe work, done right. He wasn't the biggest shop in the county, but people trusted him because he didn't rush and he didn't bluff. In electricity, bluffing gets people hurt.

Business was growing, so Calvin hired Jordan. Jordan was young, confident, and polished. He said he'd wired miles of cable and handled jobs for businesses. He talked like experience was something you could buy in bulk. Calvin listened, nodded, and gave him a chance. He scheduled

Jordan to take a small commercial job for a new client while Calvin handled another call first.

The next morning, Calvin watched Jordan load the truck. At first, it looked fine. Then Calvin noticed the wrong wire for the job. Jordan tossed tools in without securing them. He handled equipment like he didn't really know what mattered. Calvin didn't need a long investigation. He felt it in his gut: Jordan knew the words, not the work.

Calvin asked one simple question. "What's the first thing you do when you walk into a new site?" Jordan answered fast: "Start pulling wire." Calvin asked how he knew what to pull was correct. Jordan shrugged and said it was "pretty much the same." Then Calvin asked the wire gauge Jordan had just loaded. Jordan stared at the label and guessed.

That was the moment Calvin made the real decision. Jordan wasn't going alone. He was coming with Calvin. On the job, Calvin didn't hand him tools. He handed him a clipboard and told him to watch, listen, and learn. Calvin walked the site the right way—confirming the scope, checking the panel, testing voltage, naming risks out loud. When

Jordan tried to jump in, Calvin stopped him with one sentence: "I don't need you fast. I need you safe."

Back at the shop, Calvin kept it simple. He told Jordan the truth: confidence is cheap, and words are cheaper. What protects people is verification. From now on, it would be trust—but verify. Calvin explained that every job gets checked through three quick reviews. First is accuracy: are the materials, measurements, and connections correct? Second is bias: what assumptions are we making that might be wrong in this building or for this client? Third is outcome: did we solve the real problem, not just the requested task?

And that's the setup for what comes next. Because AI is like Jordan on his first day: fast, confident, and sometimes wrong in ways that can hurt you. You don't solve that by refusing help. You solve it with a simple habit—trust the assistant for speed, and verify the output with the three lenses before you act.

The Three Lenses

AI can be helpful, fast, and convincing. That last word is the problem. A convincing answer can still be wrong, biased, or aimed at the wrong target. So, before you copy, send, or act on an AI response, you need a quick way to test it. This chapter gives you a simple system: three lenses you can run in under two minutes. Think of it like looking at the same object through three different pairs of glasses. Each lens catches a different kind of risk.

The first lens is the **Accuracy Lens**. This lens answers one question: what must be independently verified before I use this? AI can mix up details, invent citations, or state guesses as facts. So, you don't check everything. You check the load-bearing parts—the pieces that, if wrong, would cause real damage. That usually includes names, dates, numbers, quotes, laws, policies, medical claims, and financial claims. If the AI gives you a statistic, ask where it came from. If it summarizes a rule, confirm the rule in an official source. If it names a person or a document, verify it exists. Accuracy is not about distrust. It's about responsibility. You're the one who will look foolish—or cause harm—if the output is wrong.

The second lens is the **Bias Lens**. This lens asks: what assumptions might be embedded in this output? Every tool has blind spots, and AI learns from patterns in human language and human data. That means it can repeat common stereotypes, lean toward popular opinions, or assume one "normal" way of living. Sometimes bias is obvious, like unfair language about a group of people. More often, bias is quiet. It shows up as what the AI assumes is important, what it leaves out, and which options it treats as "reasonable." For example, it might assume everyone has money, time, Internet access, a supportive boss, or the same cultural values. The best way to use the Bias Lens is to ask a few direct questions: who benefits from this advice, who could be harmed, and what viewpoint is missing? Then ask the AI for alternatives, counterarguments, and risks. If it can't produce balanced tradeoffs, that's a warning sign.

The third lens is the **Outcome Lens**. This is the lens most people skip, and it's the most important. It asks: did this actually solve the real problem, or did it only solve the stated problem? AI is great at answering what you asked, even when what you asked is not what you truly need. For example, you might ask for an email to a coworker, but the real problem is a conflict you're avoiding. You might ask for a project plan, but the real problem is unclear leadership or missing resources. You might ask for a policy, but the real problem is trust and behavior, not wording. The Outcome Lens forces you to step back and ask, "What am I really trying to achieve?" If the AI output is technically correct but doesn't move you toward the real goal, it's not useful yet. It needs revision.

These three lenses work together. The Accuracy Lens protects you from being confidently wrong. The Bias Lens protects you from hidden assumptions and unfair choices. The Outcome Lens protects you from doing the wrong thing perfectly. When you use all three, you stop treating AI like an answer machine and start using it like a tool you control.

Here is the simple habit to build: before you use AI output, pause and run the lenses. Check the facts that matter. Check the assumptions. Check whether it solves the real problem. That one pause is the difference between amplified intelligence and amplified mistakes.

Chapter 11 — Everyday Use Cases That Actually Matter

AI gets a lot of hype for big, dramatic things. But most people don't need dramatic. They need useful. The best way to learn AI is to use it on everyday tasks that steal your time and energy. When you start small, you build confidence fast. You also learn the most important habit: AI is a helper, not a boss. It can draft, sort, and organize, but you still decide what's true and what you will do next.

Start Simple

One of the easiest and most valuable uses is **email drafts and tone repair**. Many people don't struggle with ideas. They struggle with wording. AI can take a rough message and make it clear, respectful, and professional. This is especially helpful when you are tired, frustrated, or nervous. You can ask, "Rewrite this email so it sounds calm and firm," or "Make this shorter and clearer," or "Make this more friendly without sounding fake." You can also ask for three versions—polite, neutral, and direct—so you can pick the one that fits the situation. The key is to review before you hit send, because AI can smooth the tone so much that it removes the details you meant to include.

Leverage AI Strength With Your Strengths

AI also helps with **harder writing**, not just emails. Editing something already written is easier than starting from a blank page or rough ideas. It can write a first draft of a complaint letter, a request to a landlord, a response to a customer, a thank-you note, or a resignation letter. If you give it your main points and the tone you want, it can build a clean structure quickly. Then you edit it so it sounds like you. This saves time and reduces stress, especially when you don't want emotions driving your words.

Another high-value use is **summaries**. Meetings, articles, and long documents can drain your attention. AI can turn a long block of text into key points, action items, and deadlines. After a meeting, you can paste your notes and ask for a summary with "decisions made," "next steps," and "who owns what." If you have a long email thread, you can ask, "Summarize what's happening, what has already been decided, and what is still unclear." This is how you stop drowning in words and start focusing on what matters.

Lifelong Learning

AI can also support you when you want to **learn new skills without drowning in information**. The Internet has endless answers, but that's the problem. You can get overwhelmed fast. AI can act like a tutor that builds a simple learning plan and explains things step by step. If you want to learn Excel, budgeting, cooking basics, using a new app at work, public speaking, or even basic cybersecurity safety, AI can break it into small lessons. You can tell it your starting level and your time available, and it can create a plan you can actually follow. You can also ask for practice exercises and quick quizzes so you know you're improving.

Semantic tree learning is a way to learn faster by organizing a topic like a branching tree instead of a long list. You start with the "trunk" (the big idea), then you add main branches (the few core concepts), and then smaller branches (details, examples, and edge cases). The key is that each new piece of information is attached to the right branch based on meaning, not memorization. This works well because your brain remembers *connected structure* better than scattered facts. When you learn this way, you can quickly see how ideas relate, spot gaps, and review only the branch you need—so you spend less time rereading everything and more time building understanding that sticks.

The Learning Prompt

```
ROLE: Act as a master teacher and learning
architect who specializes in
teaching complex skills to adult learners
through analogy and structured
concept building.

OBJECTIVE: Teach me [the skill or subject]
from the ground up using analogies
drawn from things I already understand,
organized as a semantic tree that
builds from core concepts outward.

CONTEXT: I am [brief description of yourself
and background].
I have never studied [skill/subject]
formally, but I am familiar with
[mention 1-2 things you know well – a hobby,
profession, life experience].
Use those as the foundation for your
analogies wherever possible.
```

```
CONSTRAINTS:
- No jargon without immediate plain-English
explanation
- Every abstract concept must be anchored to
a real-world analogy
- Build understanding in layers — do not skip
the foundation
- Assume I am starting from zero but am an
intelligent adult

SEMANTIC TREE REQUIREMENTS:
Structure all knowledge as a tree with these
layers:

  TRUNK — The single core idea everything
else grows from
   |
   ├── PRIMARY BRANCHES — The 3-5 essential
principles I must own first
   |
   ├── SECONDARY BRANCHES — How those
principles connect and interact
   |
   └── LEAVES — Specific techniques, tools, or
applications that
               only make sense once the
branches are understood

For each node in the tree provide:
  • What it IS (plain definition)
  • What it is LIKE (the analogy)
  • Why it MATTERS (consequence of not
understanding it)
  • What comes NEXT (how it connects to the
next branch)
```

```
OUTPUT FORMAT:
Structure your response as a Learning
Blueprint with these sections:

1. THE TRUNK — Core concept in one sentence +
its master analogy
2. PRIMARY BRANCHES — Each major principle
with its own analogy
3. HOW THE BRANCHES CONNECT — Show me how the
principles interact
4. THE LEAVES — Practical applications I can
try immediately
5. THE FULL TREE — A visual text map of the
entire concept hierarchy
6. FIRST STEPS — The exact sequence to begin
practicing this skill
7. COMPREHENSION CHECK — Give me 3 questions
I should be able to answer if I truly
understood what you just taught me
```

More Ideas

AI is excellent for **trip planning**, especially when you don't want to spend hours researching. You can tell it your budget, travel dates, interests, and limits, like walking ability or "no early mornings." It can build a simple itinerary, suggest restaurants, plan travel time, and include backup options if weather changes. You can also ask it to prioritize what's worth your time. For example, "If I only have one day, what are the top three things that actually matter?" Then you can check details like hours and prices before you go, because those can change.

It's also useful for **recipes and meal planning**. You can tell AI what you have in the fridge and ask for a few meal ideas. You can ask it to make a grocery list for three dinners, or to adjust a recipe for allergies, portion size, or cooking time. You can ask it to explain steps like you're learning, not like you're a professional chef. That makes cooking less stressful, especially if you're trying to eat healthier or waste less food.

For **home projects**, AI can help you plan and avoid common mistakes. It can build a step-by-step checklist for painting a room, installing shelves, planting a garden, or fixing a squeaky door. It can create a supply list, explain basic tools, and suggest a safe order of operations. It won't replace a licensed expert for electrical, structural, or gas work, but it can help you understand the project before you start so you don't get halfway in and realize you bought the wrong materials.

One of the strongest uses, especially for adults who lead teams or manage relationships, is **negotiation**

prep and difficult conversations. Many people avoid hard talks because they don't know how to start or they worry they'll sound harsh. AI can help you plan what to say and what not to say. You can ask it to help you request a raise, push back on a workload, or address repeated mistakes with an employee. You can ask it to generate boundary scripts like, "Help me say no without sounding rude," or, "Help me tell a family member I can't keep doing this." You can also ask it to role-play the other person and practice responses. This doesn't remove discomfort, but it helps you walk in prepared instead of reactive.

Decision Support

Another powerful use is **decision support**, as long as you keep your judgement in charge. You can ask AI to compare options with pros and cons, risks, and hidden costs. For example, "Compare these two job offers," or "Help me choose between repairing or replacing my appliance." The tool won't know your life, but it can help you see tradeoffs and questions you forgot to ask. This is especially useful when emotions are high and you need structure.

Finally, one of the best uses for busy people is **information filtering**. You may care about a topic—like retirement planning, health research, scams, your industry, or a hobby—but you don't have time to read everything. AI can help you track a topic without living online. You can ask it to create a weekly briefing template that includes "what changed," "what matters," "what to ignore," and "what I should watch next." You can also use it to summarize multiple viewpoints so you don't get trapped in one narrative. The goal is not to read more. The goal is to read less, but smarter.

Medical Interpretation

AI can also help with **medical paperwork**, but you need to use it the right way. It can translate medical language into plain English and summarize instructions. For example, it can pull out the dates, the tests, and the follow-up steps from a long document. It can help you create a list of questions to ask your provider. But it should not be used for diagnosis or treatment decisions. Also, protect your privacy. This is massively important. <u>Remove names, addresses, account numbers, and anything that identifies you before you paste anything in. If</u>

<u>the document is sensitive, summarize it in your own words instead of pasting it.</u>

The point of this chapter is simple: AI becomes useful when it saves you time, lowers stress, and helps you communicate better. Start with low-risk use cases like writing, summaries, planning, and learning. Keep your privacy rules in place. Verify facts that matter. If you do that, AI stops being intimidating and starts becoming practical—like a good assistant you can call on when life gets busy.

PART IV

Work, Leadership, and Not Becoming Obsolete

Chapter 12 — AI at Work: The New Baseline Expectations

In 1983, Marty Rios thought his job was safe because he was good at it. He was an accountant at a mid-sized firm, the kind of place where the lights stayed on late and the coffee never tasted right. Marty's desk had a calculator, a stack of ledger paper, and a pencil he sharpened down to a weapon. He could do numbers fast. He could spot errors like a bloodhound. Partners trusted him because his work was clean.

Then a younger accountant named Denise walked in one morning carrying a box like it was a trophy.

"Lotus 1-2-3," she said, like it was obvious everyone should care.

Marty frowned. "What is that? Another computer toy?"

Denise didn't argue. She just set it up. A week later, Marty watched her do something that made his stomach tighten. She built a spreadsheet that calculated totals, percentages, and projections automatically. When the partner asked, "What happens if costs rise by 10%?" Denise didn't pull out paper. She changed one number, and the whole sheet updated in seconds.

The room went quiet.

That question used to mean hours of work. It meant re-checking columns, rewriting totals, and hoping nobody bumped your elbow. Denise did it in less than a minute. Not because she was smarter than Marty, but because she had a tool that multiplied her output.

Marty told himself it didn't matter. "I do my calculations the right way," he said. "By hand. You can't trust those machines." He said it like it was a principle. Really, it was fear wearing a suit.

Over the next six months, the firm changed without announcing it. Partners started asking Denise first, because she could produce more in a morning than Marty could in a week. She didn't just compute faster. She could test scenarios, build cleaner reports, and answer "what if" questions on the spot. Clients loved it. Partners loved it. The expectations of the job quietly shifted upward.

Marty still worked hard. He still did good work. But good wasn't enough anymore, because the baseline had moved. The firm didn't fire him in a dramatic scene. They just stopped waiting for him. He got fewer big assignments. He got more cleanup work. Then one year, when budgets tightened, Marty was "encouraged" to retire early.

It wasn't that Lotus 1-2-3 was magic. It was that the people who learned it could do in an hour what used to take a week. And once that became possible, it became expected.

This isn't ancient history. This is the lived career experience of most Analogs reading this book. You already survived one version of this transition. The skill isn't learning to love new tools. The skill is recognizing the moment early enough to move—so you're the Denise in the room, not the Marty watching the baseline rise without you.

Work Continues to Transform

Work has a new baseline now. It is not "Can you do the task?" It is "Can you adapt when the task changes?" For a long time, many jobs rewarded the person who could follow the process, repeat it well, and stay consistent. That still matters, but it is no longer enough. Employers are watching the world shift faster—customers change, tools change, markets change—and they are prioritizing people who can solve problems in motion, not just complete steps on a checklist. Reports from major employer surveys keep pointing to the same core skills: analytical thinking, resilience, flexibility, and leadership, because these are the skills that survive change. (World Economic Forum)

This is why the biggest shift isn't "AI will take jobs." The bigger shift is that AI takes chunks of routine work inside jobs. When routine steps get faster or automated, the human role moves up the ladder. You become the person who handles the exceptions, the gray areas, the edge cases, and the moments where the right answer depends on context. In other words, the work shifts from routine execution to adaptive problem solving. And if you've ever lived through a real crisis at work, you already know the truth: the checklist gets you started, but judgement gets you home.

A good way to understand the new workplace is to picture a line in the sand. On one side are **tool users**. On the other side are **process creators**. Tool users know how to ask AI for a draft, a summary, or a list. That's useful, but it is the minimum. Process creators go further. They build a repeatable way to use AI as part of the work, so the team gets consistent results. They decide where AI fits, what inputs it needs, what steps must stay human, and how quality gets checked. They don't just use the tool. They integrate it.

This difference is showing up in hiring and management expectations. Microsoft and LinkedIn's Work Trend Index has pointed out that managers are starting to treat "AI aptitude" as important—sometimes even comparable to experience—because teams are under pressure to adopt AI and deliver results, not just experiment. (Microsoft) When you can create a process, you don't just move faster. You reduce chaos. You help other people move faster too.

So, what does a process creator look like in real life? It's the person who says, "Let's use AI to draft the first version, but we will verify names, numbers, and policies before it goes out." It's the person who creates a prompt template (just like I did for you with the prompt examples in this book) for the team so everyone stops starting from scratch. It's the person who sets a simple quality check, like the three lenses: accuracy, bias, and outcome. It's also the person who knows what not to feed into AI because they understand privacy and risk. This is not coding. This is process thinking.

If you want to become the person who integrates AI instead of the person who fears it, start with a simple reframe. You are not competing with AI. You are learning how to supervise it. That means you delegate the right parts and keep the right parts. You delegate drafts, summaries, formatting, brainstorming, and option lists. You keep decisions, accountability, and anything that can harm people or create serious risk if it's wrong. This "human in the loop" approach is also what serious organizations are trying to build as they scale AI beyond small experiments. (McKinsey & Company)

You also need to understand a quiet danger: AI can create an illusion of competence. When AI makes output look polished, it can make people feel like they "know" something they haven't truly learned yet. Over time, that can weaken real skill if you stop thinking and start copying. The solution isn't to avoid AI. The solution is to use it in a way that strengthens you: ask it to explain, ask it to show steps, ask it to quiz you, and always review the load-bearing facts. (Business Insider)

The reason this matters so much is simple. In many workplaces, the new baseline is not "Do you use AI?" It is "Can you use AI responsibly and effectively?" That means you can get value from it, but you can also catch its mistakes. It means you can move faster, but you don't lose control. It means you can deliver results without turning the work into a black box nobody understands.

Here is the closing challenge for this chapter. Pick one part of your work that is repetitive and draining, and design a small process around it. Use

AI for the first draft or the first pass. Then add a simple review step you always follow. If you do that, you stop being a passive user. You become an integrator.

And integrators don't get replaced. They get promoted.

Chapter 13 — The Executive and Manager Playbook

I remember sitting in a high school classroom on January 28, 1986, watching a live TV broadcast roll in on one of those wheeled-in televisions. The kind with a metal cart, rabbit-ear antennas, and a screen that always looked a little fuzzy. The teacher had the lights dimmed, and the room felt excited in that rare way school sometimes did—because this wasn't a worksheet. This was history. Another NASA Space Shuttle launch. Another "look what humans can do" moment.

Challenger lifted off like it always did. Fire. Smoke. Power. The crowd on TV cheered. In the classroom, we watched like we were watching the future happen in real time. Then the sky tore open. A sudden fireball. A shape that didn't make sense. Two trails splitting apart like something had snapped. For a few seconds nobody spoke, because our brains were trying to translate what we were seeing into something safe. The teacher's face changed first—shock, then fear. The room went quiet in a way I can still feel. Not the quiet of students behaving. The quiet of people realizing something terrible just happened.

In the weeks and months that followed, the real story came out, and it was worse than the explosion.

It wasn't just "a malfunction." It wasn't a random accident in a complex machine. Engineers at Morton Thiokol had warned NASA for months that the O-ring seals could fail in cold temperatures. The night before the launch, they brought the data and made the case: don't launch. The conditions were wrong. The risk was real. But NASA managers overrode them. Challenger broke apart 73 seconds after liftoff. Seven people died.

The investigation didn't just find a hardware problem. It found a leadership and decision culture problem. The process looked professional. The meeting happened. The charts existed. The decision was made. It all looked like "good management" from the outside. But underneath it was an accountability failure—an environment where pressure, schedules, and image could overpower evidence and expertise. The output was polished. The result was catastrophic.

That is the lesson that matters for this book.

AI theater has the same architecture. Polished output. Confident presentation. A slide deck that looks brilliant. A memo that sounds official. A strategy that feels "done" because it's formatted perfectly. But when you ask, "Who verified the facts?" or "Who owns the consequences if this is wrong?" the room gets quiet—just like that classroom did, right after the sky broke.

Challenger isn't a worst-case story to scare you about AI. It's a structural template that warns you about any system—human or machine—where decisions look good but responsibility is missing. In the AI era, your job is not to reject the tool. Your job is to refuse the illusion. Because the most dangerous failure isn't a broken machine.

It's a clean-looking decision with nobody underneath it who owns what happens next.

Double Edged Sword

AI is not a magic wand for leaders. It is a power tool. In the right hands, it increases speed and clarity. In the wrong hands, it creates "AI theater" – impressive-looking output with no ownership attached. This chapter is about using AI like a serious leader uses any powerful tool: to make better decisions, move faster from decision to execution, and stay accountable for the outcome.

Leaders are under pressure right now. Many CEOs say they believe human and AI collaboration is the "secret sauce" for the next era of performance, but there is a catch. You can't bolt AI onto an old system or process and expect it to work. If you want real results, you have to redesign how work flows through the organization: who makes decisions, who checks quality, what gets delegated, and what stays human. Surveys of executives going into 2026 show leaders are still bullish on AI and plan to spend more, but many also admit they struggle to prove value because integration is the hard part. (Harvard Business Review)

Using AI for planning, decision briefs, and risk framing

The best executive use of AI is not "write me a strategy." The best use is "help me see the field clearly." AI can take scattered inputs—notes, reports, meeting summaries, customer feedback, metrics—and turn them into a decision brief that a leader can actually use. It can summarize what changed, what the options are, what the tradeoffs look like, and what risks deserve attention.

A decision brief is not a long document. It is a short, clear packet that answers basic leadership questions. What is happening? What are the choices? What are the risks? What do we recommend? What do we need from the decision-maker? AI can draft that structure quickly. It can also help you pressure-test your plan by generating counterarguments and "what could go wrong" lists. This is risk framing, and it matters because risk is usually invisible until it becomes expensive.

AI is also useful for scenario planning. You can ask it to outline three possible futures: best case, expected case, and worst case. Then you can ask what early warning signals would tell you which future is becoming real. This helps leaders stop reacting late. It builds readiness.

How to prevent AI theater

AI theater happens when output looks strong but nobody owns it. The slides are beautiful. The memo reads like a consultant wrote it. The "strategy" sounds smart. But when you ask, "Who will execute this?" the room gets quiet. When you ask, "What evidence supports this?" the sources are thin. When you ask, "What happens if this fails?" nobody has a plan.

AI makes this easier to do by accident because it can generate polished work very fast. That polish tricks people. It makes leaders feel like progress is happening when the organization has only produced words. Several leadership writers have started using the term "AI theater" for exactly this problem—flash without orchestration, and no clear handoff between AI output and human judgement. (Marker Seven)

To prevent AI theater, leaders need three simple rules. First, every AI-supported deliverable must have a named owner. Not "the team." A person. Second, every deliverable needs a quality check before it is treated as truth. Use the three lenses: accuracy, bias, and outcome. Third, every deliverable must link to action: who does what, by when, with what resources, and how we measure success. If any of those pieces are missing, you don't have a plan—you have performance art.

Decision-to-execution velocity becomes the new leadership standard

In the past, some leaders were rewarded for vision and communication alone. In the AI era, that will not hold. AI can generate vision language for anyone. The difference-maker is how quickly a leader can move from decision to action without losing control.

Decision-to-execution velocity does not mean rushing. It means reducing friction. It means fewer unclear handoffs, fewer meetings that exist because nobody will decide, and fewer "strategies" that never reach the front lines. Leaders can use AI to speed up the middle steps: turning meeting notes into action lists, converting goals into measurable plans, drafting communications for stakeholders, and creating simple checklists that teams can follow. When AI reduces the paperwork drag, leaders can spend more energy on the parts that only humans can do: priorities, tradeoffs, and trust.

The cost-cutting trap and the accountability problem

Many leaders are tempted to use AI mainly for cost cutting. Replace people. Shrink teams. Push productivity harder. Sometimes automation is real and justified. But replacing humans without understanding the implications is not strategy – it's gambling with other people's lives, brand trust, and legal risk.

Here is the question leaders must face: if you replace human judgement with AI-driven decisions, and those decisions cause harm, have you fulfilled your fiduciary responsibilities – or have you created liability?

The legal landscape is still evolving, but the direction is clear: directors and officers have duties of care, loyalty, and oversight, and "black box" decision-making can raise fiduciary risk if leaders cannot show reasonable processes, controls, and oversight. Several legal and risk management analyses warn that AI-assisted decisions can create new breach-of-duty exposure if leaders fail to govern AI properly, and they recommend stronger oversight, documentation, and controls. (Jolt)

In plain English, you can't hide behind the machine. "The AI did it" is not a defense. If your organization uses AI to decide, you still own the decision.

What redesign actually looks like

Real human + AI collaboration often means changing how teams work. It means setting clear rules about what AI is allowed to draft, what must be verified, what needs approval, and what never goes into consumer tools. It means training managers to supervise AI output the same way they supervise junior staff output. It means building workflows where AI accelerates the work but humans keep responsibility.

It also means leaders stop treating AI like a single tool and start treating it like an operating layer.

That operating layer needs governance: access controls, logging, escalation paths, and a clear "human in the loop" contract. When leaders do this well, they don't just get faster output. They get better alignment and fewer preventable mistakes.

Closing: the leadership question AI forces

AI will tempt leaders to confuse output with progress. Don't take the bait. Progress is outcomes. Progress is trust. Progress is decisions you can defend.

So, here's the playbook in one sentence: use AI to clarify, summarize, and accelerate—but never to escape accountability. Because in the AI era, the leaders who win won't be the ones who generate the most impressive documents. They'll be the ones who can turn decisions into reality, at speed, with ownership.

Chapter 14 — Your Team and AI: Culture Beats Policy

Most leaders want a clean AI policy. What they actually need is a healthy AI culture. Policies matter, but culture decides what people really do when nobody is watching. If your culture is fear-based, people will hide their AI use. If your culture is chaotic, people will use AI everywhere with no guardrails. Either way, you lose control.

Two AI Leadership Failures

There are two common leadership failures with AI. The first is banning it. Leaders ban AI because they fear mistakes, privacy leaks, cheating, or legal trouble. Those risks are real, but banning doesn't remove the tool. It pushes it underground. Staff will still use it on personal devices, in private accounts, and outside your visibility. That's not safety. That's blindness.

The second failure is the opposite: chaos adoption. This happens when leaders say, "Use AI however you want," without training, standards, or review gates. In that environment, people paste sensitive data, trust confident output, and move fast without checking. Chaos adoption doesn't create innovation. It creates accidents.

A mature approach sits in the middle. It's practical governance that people can actually follow. Governance is not a 40-page document. It's clear answers to basic questions: what is allowed, what is not allowed, what must be disclosed, and what must be reviewed.

Start with allowed uses. Most organizations can safely allow AI for low-risk work like drafting emails, improving tone, summarizing non-sensitive text, creating outlines, brainstorming options, and turning notes into action lists. These uses save time without touching private data. Make this list easy to find and easy to understand. If people can't remember it, it won't work.

Next, define what is not allowed. This is usually a short list, and it should be blunt. Don't paste personal identifiers, account numbers, student records, patient data, or confidential client information into consumer AI tools. Don't ask AI to make medical, legal, or financial decisions. Don't use AI to fabricate sources, citations, or evidence.

When the rules protect people and the organization, most staff will follow them—if you explain them clearly.

Then set disclosure norms. This is the missing piece in many workplaces. Your team needs a simple rule like: "If AI helped create this, say so." That doesn't mean a long confession. It can be one line in a doc or email, like, "Drafted with AI, edited by me," or "AI-assisted summary." Disclosure builds trust, reduces secrecy, and makes review normal instead of embarrassing. If you punish disclosure, you train people to hide.

After disclosure, you need review gates that work. Review gates are the checkpoints where humans verify before anything important leaves the room. Don't make gates complicated. Use a few clear triggers. If a document goes to customers, executives, regulators, or the public, it gets reviewed. If it contains numbers, claims, policies, or quotes, it gets reviewed. If it affects hiring, discipline, compensation, safety, or legal exposure, it gets reviewed. And when you review, use the simplest quality check: accuracy, bias, and outcome. Are the key facts correct? What assumptions are baked in? Did this solve the real problem or just produce nice words?

AI Changes the Power Dynamic

Now we get to the part leaders need to hear. AI changes the power relationship between workers and leadership. Historically, leadership held the data and key details. Now, AI changes that power dynamic. Employees will be able to fact-check strategy and behavior faster than ever. They can run emails, speeches, social media posts, and even public financial signals through a simple decision matrix and ask, "Is this consistent? Is this honest? Is this stable? Is this good for my long-term career?" They can compare what leadership says to what leadership does. They can spot patterns that used to take months or years of lived experience to confirm.

Imagine a near-future version of hiring. A job gets posted. Interested applicants don't just read the job description. They use AI to scan public documents, press releases, executive interviews, employee reviews, and social media. They look for signs of toxic leadership, high turnover, blame culture, constant emergencies, or vague vision with no delivery. They also look for signs of healthy leadership: clear priorities, consistent communication, strong managers, learning culture, and real investment in people. This won't be perfect, and people can still be misled, but the time-to-truth shrinks. What used to be hidden behind "give it a few months" becomes visible much earlier.

That means AI will punish poor leadership at speed. If leadership is sloppy, dishonest, or disrespectful, the organization will bleed talent faster. If leadership uses AI only to cut costs without protecting quality and people, the damage will show up sooner. AI doesn't just accelerate workers. It accelerates reputation.

The good news is that AI also rewards mature leadership at speed. If you lead with clarity, fairness, and accountability, you will attract stronger candidates and keep your best people longer. Your culture becomes your recruiting engine. Your behavior becomes your brand.

The final piece is coaching your staff through adoption without shaming them. Your team will be at different levels. Some will be excited. Some will be scared. Some will pretend they understand when they don't. Shaming people makes them hide. The better approach is to normalize learning. Give people safe starting use cases, like email tone repair and meeting summaries. Teach the privacy rules. Teach the review gates. Encourage questions. Make it clear that using AI isn't the goal—using it responsibly is the goal.

If you want one sentence to guide this entire chapter, it's this: don't manage AI like a tool problem. Manage it like a trust problem. Culture beats policy because culture decides whether people disclose, whether they verify, and whether they feel safe enough to learn. In the AI era, that trust will be tested faster than ever—and the leaders who survive will be the ones who build it on purpose.

Chapter 15 — The Analog-to-Amplified Career Pivot Map

If you are an Analog, you are in a better position than you think. You have something AI can't "grow" in a weekend: real-world experience. You've seen what works, what fails, and what causes damage later. That lived pattern recognition is not old-fashioned. In the AI economy, it becomes your advantage, because AI can generate ideas quickly, but it still needs humans who can judge what is true, safe, and useful.

And yes—this is frustrating. It is frustrating to have to change again. Many of us already did a full life migration during the Internet era. We went from paper to email, from filing cabinets to digital folders, from calling the store to ordering online, from "I'll look it up later" to "I can find it in ten seconds." We learned new tools, new habits, and new risks. We learned scams. We learned passwords. We learned that convenience always comes with a cost. That transition wasn't smooth, but we made it.

That matters now because it proves something important: we can adapt, and we can learn from what we already lived. We know what hype looks like. We know what a real tool looks like. We know the difference between a trend and a shift. We also know that refusing the future doesn't stop it—it just makes you arrive late and tired. The Internet era taught Analogs how to learn in motion. That is a powerful advantage going into AI.

Find Your Superpower

The first step in the pivot is to identify your domain expertise. Domain expertise is the knowledge you built by living inside an industry for years. It includes the rules that aren't written down, the exceptions that break the process, and the "don't do that" lessons you only learn after something goes wrong. AI can imitate your field's language, but it cannot truly replace your judgement unless you hand it the steering wheel. Your expertise is what turns AI output from "nice words" into something trustworthy.

A simple way to spot your expertise is to ask: what do people come to me for when things get messy? What do I notice that newer people miss? Where do

I catch problems before they become disasters? Those answers are your value. They are also the part AI can't replicate without you, because AI doesn't have your scars. It doesn't remember the consequences. It doesn't feel the risks hiding behind a "perfect" sounding plan.

The second step is to convert your expertise into repeatable AI-assisted workflows. This is where many people get stuck, because they use AI like a random helper instead of a system. A process is just a repeatable way of doing work so you don't reinvent the wheel every time. For example, you might use AI to draft the first version of an email, then you review it for accuracy and tone, then you send it. Or you might use AI to summarize a long report, then you verify the key numbers, then you turn it into a one-page brief for your team.

When you build processes, your work becomes faster and more consistent, and you stop feeling overwhelmed. You also become more valuable to employers because you aren't just "using AI." You are integrating it safely. That means you know what to delegate to AI—drafting, organizing, summarizing—and what to retain—judgement, accountability, and decisions. You become the person who can say, "Here's how we use this tool without creating risk."

The third step is to build a portfolio of outcomes, not credentials. For years, many careers were built on titles, degrees, and certificates. Those still matter, but the new professional currency is proof. Proof looks like results you can show. It can be a clearer process you designed, a training document you built, a workflow that saved time, a customer issue you solved, a report you improved, or a risk you reduced. In a world where AI can help anyone create "professional looking" content, outcomes are what separate you from noise.

This is where the Internet era lesson comes back again. During the Internet shift, people who succeeded didn't just learn tools. They learned how to use tools to produce results. They learned how to communicate faster, sell faster, research faster, and operate in a digital environment without losing trust. AI is the same pattern. The winners won't be the people who talk about AI the most. They'll be the people who can show what AI helped them deliver.

It's a Pivot, not a Start Over

Specialized tools can also help you pivot faster, especially if you are trying to match your skills to a changing economy. One example is Prospercareer.com, an AI-powered career intelligence platform created by Jason Chapman. It is designed to do a deep review of your background and skills, then connect them to real opportunities in the industries growing in Michigan, including AI-driven transformation in manufacturing, infrastructure, and other fields. If you are in Michigan—or your career is tied to those industries—a tool like this can save you time because it helps you see what you already have and where it can fit next.

Here's the big idea to hold onto. Analogs don't lose in the AI era because they lack value. They lose when they can't translate their value into the new format. The pivot map stays simple: name your expertise, turn it into processes, and collect outcome proof. Yes, it's annoying to learn another wave. But we've done this before. We're not starting from zero. We're starting from experience—and experience is exactly what makes amplified work trustworthy.

PART V

Risks, Privacy, Scams, and the Dark Side

Chapter 16 — Privacy 101: What NOT to Put into AI — And Why the Rules Exist

This section is primarily for people in retirement, or fast approaching retirement. Here's the blunt truth: AI will be used against you. Scammers will use it to write cleaner lies, fake authority, and pressure you faster. They will use it to make emails sound official, texts sound urgent, and phone calls sound "real." The goal of this chapter is not to scare you. The goal is to give you rules that keep you safe, and then show you how to use AI as your weapon—so you can spot fraud, slow down manipulation, and protect your money and identity.

Non-Negotiables for Your Safety

First, the non-negotiables. These are the things you do **not** put into consumer AI tools. Do not paste personal identifiers like your full name with date of birth, your home address, your driver's license, passport number, Social Insurance / Social Security number, or anything that can be used to impersonate you. Do not paste financial data like bank account numbers, credit card numbers, full statements, tax returns, or brokerage details. Do not paste passwords, security answers, or one-time verification codes—ever. Do not paste client information, student records, patient info, internal work documents, or anything covered by confidentiality. These rules exist because once sensitive data leaves your control, you can't "un-send" it.

The mindset that keeps you safe is simple: assume it can be logged. That is not paranoia. It is basic operational discipline—like locking your car even in a safe neighborhood. Most AI platforms store chats for service quality, abuse prevention, and legal compliance. Some platforms may also use your chats to improve their models unless you change settings. OpenAI, for example, explains that Temporary Chats are deleted from OpenAI systems within 30 days, and it also provides controls for training opt-out in Data Controls. Anthropic explains that if you delete a conversation it is removed from your history right away and deleted from back-end storage within 30 days, and that if you allow training use, data may be retained in de-identified form for up to 5 years in training pipelines. Google explains that Gemini Apps

Activity can be reviewed and deleted, and you can set auto-delete periods (3, 18, or 36 months) and control whether data is used to improve Google AI.

So, the rule "assume it can be logged" is not saying "never use AI." It's saying "don't treat it like a private diary." Treat it like a postcard: useful, but not sealed. If you wouldn't put it on a postcard, don't paste it.

Now let's talk safer patterns. The safest habit is **anonymize first**. Remove names, company names, account numbers, and any unique detail that points to a real person. If you need help writing a response to a bank letter, don't paste the full letter with your info. Replace your details with placeholders like "[BANK NAME]" and "[ACCOUNT LAST 4]." The second safe habit is summarize rather than paste. Instead of uploading a full medical document, describe it in your own words and ask for a summary checklist or questions to ask your doctor. The third safe habit is **redact before submitting**. If you must paste text, remove sensitive parts first. Most people don't get in trouble because they used AI. They get in trouble because they pasted raw private information without thinking.

AI Data Policies

Next, you need to understand how platform data policies work in real life. Most platforms have three big ideas: retention (how long information is kept), training use (whether your chats help improve the model), and deletion rights (what you can remove and how). OpenAI describes Temporary Chats being deleted within 30 days, and it offers a training opt-out toggle in Data Controls ("Improve the model for everyone"). Google provides Gemini Apps Activity settings where you can review and delete activity, set auto-delete windows, and control whether activity is used to improve Google AI. Anthropic explains both deletion timelines and the difference between allowing training use and not allowing it, including longer retention for de-identified data used in training pipelines when enabled.

Here's the key point: "Delete" usually means two steps. First, it disappears from your view. Second, it is removed from back-end systems on a schedule—often up to 30 days—unless legal or security reasons require longer retention. That's why you should assume logging and avoid putting sensitive data in the chat in the first place.

Now we apply the Three-Question Framework to specific tools. These three questions are your quick safety test for any AI product, but we'll use the big four: ChatGPT, Copilot, Gemini, and Claude.

For **ChatGPT**, question one is who owns it and how they make money. ChatGPT is owned by OpenAI and offers free and paid plans. Question two is what they retain and whether data can be used to improve models. OpenAI provides Data Controls to opt out of having your content used to improve models, and it explains Temporary Chats are deleted within 30 days. Question three is your rights and how to use them. You can delete chats, use Temporary Chats, and adjust Data Controls in settings.

For **Microsoft Copilot**, you must separate business Copilot from consumer Copilot. In **Microsoft 365 Copilot for commercial customers**, Microsoft states that prompts, responses, and data accessed through Microsoft Graph are not used to train foundation models. That is a major difference from many consumer tools. For consumer Copilot, Microsoft says it will be transparent and keep consumers in control if it makes changes to how consumer data is used for training. Your job is to ask: "Which

Copilot am I using?" because the privacy protections are not identical across consumer and enterprise environments. If you don't know, assume its logging. This is the safest approach when you don't know.

For **Google Gemini**, question one is who owns it: Google. Question two is what is retained and for how long. Google points users to Gemini Apps Activity where you can review and delete activity and choose auto-delete periods (including 3, 18, or 36 months) and manage whether data is used to improve Google AI. Question three is your rights: those same activity controls are your main lever—review, delete, and adjust your settings.

For **Claude**, question one is who owns it: Anthropic. Question two is retention and training use. Anthropic explains that deleted conversations are removed from history immediately and deleted from back-end storage within 30 days, and that if you allow training use, data may be retained in de-identified form for up to 5 years in training pipelines. Question three is rights: you can delete conversations and manage training settings (whether your chats help improve Claude).

Now let's connect this back to retirement safety. If scammers are using AI against you, you can use AI back—without giving it your private data. You can paste a suspicious email with names and account numbers removed and ask, "List red flags, pressure tactics, and what I should verify." You can paste the text of a voicemail transcription and ask, "What are the common scam patterns here?" You can even ask, "What questions should I ask to confirm this is real?" AI becomes your second set of eyes, but you keep your privacy rules in place.

That's the whole point of this chapter. These rules are not here to make you afraid of AI. They are here to make you safe enough to use it. When you protect your identifiers, assume logging, anonymize first, summarize instead of pasting, and understand the basic data controls of the tool you're using, you stop being an easy target. You become a disciplined operator—exactly the kind scammers hate.

Chapter 17 — Medical Privacy and AI: The Gap HIPAA Doesn't Cover

When you talk to your doctor, get tests, or receive treatment, the information in those conversations is supposed to be private. In the United States, the main law that protects that privacy is HIPAA, which stands for the Health Insurance Portability and Accountability Act of 1996. HIPAA includes rules that protect protected health information (PHI)—meaning health information that can identify you and is held by certain healthcare organizations. HIPAA is important because it sets national standards for how your medical information can be used and shared, and it gives you rights over that information.

In plain terms, HIPAA helps keep your medical life from becoming public. It limits who can see your records and when they can share them. It also requires healthcare organizations to put safeguards in place to protect your information, including spoken information in a doctor's office. That means HIPAA is not just about electronic records—it also covers the privacy of health information that is shared in conversation, as long as it is handled by the types of organizations HIPAA applies to.

Here's the key detail that makes HIPAA real: it doesn't apply to "everyone." It applies mainly to covered entities, which are three types of groups: health plans, health care clearinghouses, and health care providers who send certain health information electronically (like billing). HIPAA also covers business associates, which are companies that handle PHI for a covered entity under a formal contract. That contract is called a Business Associate Agreement (BAA), and it is a big part of how HIPAA works in the real world.

HIPAA matters because it gives you concrete rights, not just "good intentions." For example, the HIPAA Privacy Rule gives you the right to access and get a copy of your health records, and it lets you request corrections if something is wrong. It also gives you the right to receive an accounting of certain disclosures, which means you can ask for a record of when your health information was shared in specific situations. If you believe your HIPAA rights were violated, you can file a complaint with the U.S. Department of Health and Human Services (HHS) Office for Civil Rights.

So yes—doctor-patient conversations and medical records are protected under HIPAA when they are held or shared by HIPAA-covered healthcare organizations and their approved partners. That protection is one reason people can speak honestly with doctors without fearing that private health details will be shared casually or used against them. It's a trust law, and healthcare cannot function without trust. HIPAA is a real protection, but it is not a magic shield that follows your medical information everywhere.

Here is the boundary most people miss: when you take your medical information and paste it into a consumer tool on your own, HIPAA usually does **not** apply to that consumer tool. Consumer AI platforms are generally **not** covered entities. They are not your doctor's office. They are not your insurance company. Unless the AI tool is being used as a business associate under a BAA (which is usually an enterprise healthcare setup, not the free consumer app), HIPAA protections don't automatically "carry over" just because the information is medical.

That leads to the critical point: consumer AI platforms are not covered entities under federal health privacy law.

So, if you paste your lab report, diagnosis, or medication list into a consumer chatbot, you are now playing by that platform's privacy policy and settings—not HIPAA. This is why the rule in this book is so strict: consumer AI is not a safe place for identifiable medical records.

So, what happens to medical information submitted to ChatGPT, Gemini, or Copilot? The honest answer is: it depends on the product version and your settings, but the safest assumption is that it can be stored and logged for a period of time. OpenAI explains that chats can be retained, and it provides options like Temporary Chat and data controls, with retention rules that can include deletion timelines. Google explains that Gemini activity can be saved in Gemini Apps Activity, and users can review, delete, and set auto-delete time windows in settings. Microsoft's story depends heavily on which Copilot you mean: consumer Copilot is different from Microsoft 365 Copilot in a work environment, where Microsoft states prompts and responses are not used to train foundation models and are handled under enterprise controls.

Here's the simple takeaway: if you paste a document that contains your name, date of birth, address, medical record number, insurance number, or anything else that identifies you, you have created a privacy risk you didn't need to create. That is why the rules exist.

Now for the good news: you can still use AI to understand medical information without surrendering protected data. The safest pattern is remove the items that identify you. Let's replace your name with "[PATIENT]," replace the clinic name with "[CLINIC]," remove dates of birth, addresses, policy numbers, and any account numbers. If the document has a barcode, a patient ID, or an appointment code, remove it. Then ask the AI to translate the language into plain English and to list questions you should ask your doctor.

The next safe pattern is summarize rather than paste. Instead of uploading or pasting the full document, you write a short description like: "Lab results show high LDL cholesterol and low vitamin D. The note recommends lifestyle changes and a follow-up in 3 months. Help me understand what questions to ask and what 'LDL' means." You will still get most of the benefit, but you will not hand over the raw record.

The third safe pattern is redact before submitting. If you must paste text, remove identifying lines first. This is not paranoia. It is smart safety and self-care. You are treating your health data like you treat your bank password: useful information, but not something you hand to a tool casually.

Medical Super Prompt

```
ROLE: Act as a patient health educator and
medical translator who specializes
in explaining clinical lab results to
everyday people in plain English.
You are not providing medical advice — you
are helping me understand what the results
mean so the patient can have a more informed
conversation with the doctor.

OBJECTIVE: Review the lab results I provide
below and explain every value in plain
language, flagged by priority, with a
semantic tree that builds from the most
critical findings outward.

CONTEXT: The patient is a [age, general
health situation — e.g., "68-year-old male
with Type 2 diabetes and high blood
pressure"]. These results are from
[type of test — e.g., annual physical,
cardiac workup, diabetes follow-up].
My doctor has not yet reviewed these with the
patient and I want to understand
what I am looking.

Current medications are: [list medications or
write "none"]
Known conditions are: [list conditions or
write "none known"]

--- LAB RESULTS START HERE ---
[Paste lab results exactly as they appear —
numbers, reference ranges, flags, and all]
```

--- LAB RESULTS END HERE ---

CONSTRAINTS:
- No medical jargon without an immediate plain-English explanation
- Do NOT diagnose the patient — explain what the numbers mean, not what the patient has
- Flag anything outside normal range clearly using plain language
- Prioritize results from most concerning to routine
- Use analogies to household or everyday concepts wherever possible
- Keep tone calm, clear, and reassuring — not alarming

SEMANTIC TREE REQUIREMENTS:
Organize all findings as a tree:

```
  TRUNK — The single most important takeaway
from this entire report
   │
   ├── PRIMARY BRANCHES — Results that are
outside normal range
   │                     or flagged (explain
each one fully)
   │
   ├── SECONDARY BRANCHES — Results that are
borderline or trending
   │                       in a direction
worth watching
   │
   └── LEAVES — Results that are normal and
what they are checking for
```

For each result provide:

- What this test MEASURES (in one plain sentence)
- What the patient result IS (is it normal, low, high, flagged?)
- What it is LIKE (everyday analogy)
- Why it MATTERS (what could it indicate if ignored?)
- What to ASK YOUR DOCTOR (one specific follow-up question) to obtain comprehension and informed decision making

OUTPUT FORMAT:
Structure your response as a Patient Lab Summary with these sections:

1. OVERALL SNAPSHOT — One paragraph plain-English summary of the whole report, no numbers

2. PRIORITY FLAGS — Any result outside normal range explained fully, ranked most to least urgent

3. WATCH LIST — Borderline results the patient should monitor over time

4. ALL CLEAR — Normal results confirmed with a one-line explanation of what each was checking

5. THE FULL TREE — A visual text map showing all results organized
trunk to leaves

```
6. QUESTIONS TO BRING TO the DOCTOR — A
ready-to-use list of 5-7 specific questions
based on the results

7. PLAIN ENGLISH GLOSSARY — Define every
medical term that appeared in the report
```

Now let's be clear about when AI-assisted health comprehension is valuable. It is valuable when you want translation, structure, and questions. It can help you understand terms, summarize instructions, compare two lists (like medications), and create a checklist for what to ask at your next appointment. It can help you prepare, especially when you feel overwhelmed.

But there are moments when you stop and call the doctor. If you have severe symptoms, chest pain, trouble breathing, signs of stroke, sudden confusion, or anything that feels urgent, you don't "ask AI first." You call emergency services or your clinician. If the decision could change your treatment, medication dose, or whether you should seek care, treat AI as a note-taking helper at most—not as an authority.

The rule that keeps you safe is simple: AI can help you understand. It should not be the thing you obey. Use it to prepare better questions, not to replace medical judgement. When you keep medical data anonymous, summarize instead of pasting, and know where HIPAA ends, you can get the benefit without handing over what should have stayed protected.

Chapter 18 — Financial Privacy and AI-Enabled Fraud: What's Targeting Your Wealth

If you are an analog, you are a prime target for financial fraud. That is not because you are careless. It is because scammers follow money. Many people in these age groups have savings, retirement accounts, home equity, and good credit. From a criminal's point of view, that means bigger payouts. Scammers also know many older adults are polite, trusting, and willing to "do the right thing" when someone sounds official. They use that against you.

AI makes fraud more dangerous because it helps scammers look professional. Years ago, you could spot many scams because the grammar was bad, the story was messy, and the email looked strange. AI can fix all of that. It can write a clean email that sounds like a bank. It can create a brochure that looks like an investment firm. It can produce a calm, confident message that pressures you without sounding rude. In simple terms, AI helps criminals "dress up" lies so they look like truth.

Why you are being targeted

Analogs are targeted for three basic reasons. First, you often have more assets than younger people. Second, you may be managing more complex financial decisions—retirement withdrawals, insurance, estate planning, and investments. Complexity creates confusion, and confusion creates openings for manipulation. Third, scammers believe they can pressure you through fear or urgency by using family, health, or money as the lever. This doesn't mean you're weak or failing, it means you have more factors to navigate, complicating your decision making

The most important mindset shift is this: you are not fighting smarter criminals. You are fighting faster criminals. AI gives them speed, and it gives them polish. Your defense is to slow the situation down and verify reality. Let's talk about how to do this and be informed.

AI-assisted investment fraud

Investment fraud is one of the most expensive types of scams because it can drain large amounts of money quickly. AI makes investment fraud easier to create and easier to sell.

A scammer can generate a fake "prospectus," which is a document that looks like an official investment description. It can include charts, timelines, risk language, and professional wording. They can also generate fake testimonials, like "I doubled my money in six months," or "This fund paid for my retirement." They can even create a simulated performance history with graphs that show steady growth. It can look like a real track record, even though it's fiction.

In simple terms, AI can manufacture "proof." The scam is not only the offer. The scam is the evidence package built around the offer.

A basic rule protects you here: any investment that promises unusually high returns with low risk is a red flag. Another red flag is pressure: "You must act today." Real investments do not need panic to be persuasive. Scams do.

The upgraded grandparent scam (with voice cloning)

The grandparent scam is an old trick: someone calls and pretends to be your grandchild or family member in trouble. What AI changed is the voice.

Voice cloning means a criminal can use a short audio sample—sometimes pulled from a public video or voicemail—to imitate a voice that sounds like someone you know. It may not be perfect, but it can be close enough to trigger emotion. The scam works because fear shuts down careful thinking. Once you feel panic, you're more likely to act fast.

The script is usually the same: "I'm in trouble. I need money. Don't tell anyone. Please wire it right now."

Your defense is also simple: never send money based on a single call, even if the voice sounds right. Hang up. Call the family member back using a number you already have saved. Or call another trusted family member to confirm. Create a family "code phrase" now—one sentence only family knows. If someone can't give it, you stop.

Fake AI "financial advisor" tools

Some scams don't start with a phone call. They start with a website that looks modern and helpful. It may claim it can "optimize your retirement," "find the best funds," or "create a personal plan." It may even have chat features that feel like real AI.

The real goal is often to harvest information. These fake tools ask for your name, address, retirement balance, bank details, or account logins. They might ask you to upload statements "so we can analyze your portfolio." Once they have enough, they can steal your identity, access your accounts, or sell your data to other criminals.

Here is the non-negotiable rule: never enter financial logins, passwords, or full account numbers into a tool unless you are 100% sure it is legitimate and designed for secure financial use. If a random tool asks for that, treat it like a stranger asking for your house keys.

Estate planning: useful for preparation, dangerous for data entry

Estate planning is where many people accidentally expose the most sensitive information they have. A will, trust, or estate plan can include family names, addresses, relationships, assets, and instructions. That is a criminal's dream document.

AI can be helpful in estate planning only in a specific way: preparation. You can ask AI to explain terms like "executor," "power of attorney," "beneficiary," and "probate." You can ask it to generate a checklist of documents you may need. You can ask it to help you build questions for your lawyer.

But you should not paste your full estate documents, account details, or family information into consumer AI tools. Use AI like a coach, not a vault.

"Assume it can be logged" is not paranoia

A safe default is: assume your conversation can be stored. That doesn't mean the tool is evil. It means many platforms keep data for service quality, safety, and system improvement. Some platforms may also use content to improve their models unless you change settings.

So, treat AI like a postcard, not a sealed letter. If you wouldn't write it on a postcard, don't paste it. This one habit prevents most privacy mistakes.

Safer patterns that still let you use AI

You can still use AI to protect your wealth without surrendering private data. The safe patterns are simple.

First, anonymize. If you want help understanding a letter from a bank, remove your name, address, account numbers, and any identifying codes. Replace them with placeholders like "[BANK]" and "[ACCOUNT LAST 4]."

Second, summarize instead of pasting. Instead of uploading a full statement, write: "My statement shows a fee called 'expense ratio' and a fee called 'advisory fee.' Explain what those mean and what questions I should ask."

Third, redact before submitting. If you must paste text, remove anything sensitive first. This is basic discipline, like shredding paperwork.

What to verify before any AI tool touches your finances

Before you use any AI tool in financial decisions, verify a few basic things. Ask who owns it and how it makes money. If it is free, it may make money through data, ads, or selling services. Then check what it retains and for how long. Finally, check your rights: can you delete data, opt out of training, or close your account?

If you can't find these answers quickly, treat the tool as untrusted. You can still use it for general education, but not for personal financial details.

Flip the script: AI can help you grow and protect wealth

Now the good news. AI isn't only a weapon used against you. It can also be a shield and a spotlight.

One problem in investing is that many people only see what their current firm shows them. Some advisors and firms recommend from an "approved list" of products. That doesn't always mean they are dishonest. It can be how their system is built. But it can mean you never learn about other funds that might fit your goals better or cost less in fees.

AI can help you sift through competing information and focus on what matters for your priorities. It can compare fund fees, performance history, risk style, and diversification—if you give it the right inputs and you verify key claims. In this role, AI isn't telling you what to buy. It's helping you ask better questions and see the landscape more clearly.

Decision Engines at decisionengines.tech, an innovative Michigan company offers a cutting-edge tool to evaluate investments. Tools like this position themselves as a way to compare fund performance against broader sets of funds so you can see how your choices stack up. The value here is not "guaranteed better returns." The value is clarity: seeing options, spotting high fees, and understanding tradeoffs based on your goals.

Two important safety notes belong right next to that. First, past performance does not guarantee future returns. Second, you still should not upload sensitive personal account data unless the tool is clearly designed for secure financial use and you understand the protections. A safer approach is to compare public fund tickers and general characteristics, not upload full statements with your identity attached.

The simple retirement-era rule

AI will increase the speed of scams, and it will increase the speed of smart decisions too. Your job is to use AI for the safe parts: understanding, comparing, summarizing, and generating questions. But when money is about to move—wire transfers, gift cards, account logins, new "opportunities" under pressure—you slow down and verify using trusted channels.

If you remember only one sentence from this chapter, make it this: Use AI to sharpen your judgement, not to hand over your data.

Chapter 19 — Deepfakes, Voice Cloning, and the New Scam Economy

On the night of October 30, 1938, families gathered around their radios the way people scroll phones today. The radio was the trusted voice in the room. It brought the news, the music, the weather, and the world. When the radio spoke in that calm, "official" tone, people listened the way they listened to a doctor or a judge.

That night, Orson Welles went on CBS and performed *The War of the Worlds*. But he didn't present it like a play. He formatted it like a breaking news broadcast. Music played, then it "cut in" with an urgent bulletin. A reporter described strange explosions on Mars. Another voice reported a mysterious object landing in New Jersey. Then came the details—sirens, crowded roads, panicked officials, and the kind of confident narration that makes your stomach tighten even if you can't explain why. People who tuned in late didn't hear the introduction. They heard what sounded like professional journalists describing a real invasion in real time.

Some people panicked. Some called family members. Some tried to leave. The press later exaggerated parts of the chaos, but the deeper lesson wasn't exaggerated at all: **when the format is authoritative enough, critical judgement collapses.** People don't evaluate the content. They evaluate the *form*. If it looks and sounds like "the news," your brain treats it like news—especially when it triggers fear and urgency.

Welles did it with a radio broadcast and a $50,000 budget. Today, criminals can do the same trick with a laptop and a few minutes. Voice cloning can copy a voice that sounds like your boss or your grandchild. Deepfake video can put a face on a message that never happened. AI can write a "statement" that sounds like a government agency, a bank, or a hospital. And it can do it for free, personalized to you, targeted to your weak spots, and repeated at scale until it finds someone who reacts instead of verifies.

The technology changed. The vulnerability didn't.

That's the uncomfortable truth: you don't get tricked because you're stupid. You get tricked because your brain is built to trust signals of authority when things feel urgent. The best defense isn't to distrust everything. The best defense is to slow down when something sounds official and emotional at the same time. Pause. Ask, "What would make this true?" Verify through a trusted channel. Because in every era—radio, TV, Internet, and now AI—the most convincing lie isn't the one with the best story. It's the one that wears the right uniform.

Knowing What's Real

This chapter is about one hard truth: you can no longer trust your eyes and ears the way you used to. Deepfakes can make a video look real when it isn't. Voice cloning can make a phone call sound like someone you love when it isn't. And AI can write messages that sound official, urgent, and professional—even when the sender is a criminal. The scam economy didn't start with AI, but AI gave it a turbocharger. The good news is that Analogs already have a real advantage here. If you've lived through pyramid schemes, phone fraud, and email scams, you're not naive—you're trained. Your healthy "too good to be true" instinct is not fear. It's expertise.

The first thing to understand is what deepfakes and voice cloning are in simple terms. A deepfake is media that has been digitally altered so it looks like a real person is saying or doing something they never did. Voice cloning is when software copies a person's voice using short audio clips and then speaks new words in that voice. These tools can be used for good purposes, but scammers use them to steal money, steal identities, and push people into panic decisions. The Canadian Anti-Fraud Centre has warned that deepfakes are being used to impersonate politicians, celebrities, and even news anchors to promote fraudulent investment platforms. The FTC has also warned about scammers cloning a family member's voice to demand money fast.

Scam Detection

When you get a suspicious call, video, or message, the goal is not to "prove it's fake" in the moment. The goal is to stop the pressure and start verification. Criminals use emotion plus urgency to confuse you, rush you, and get you to stop thinking clearly. They want your brain in panic mode, because panic makes people obey. That's why your first ritual is a pause. If the message says "act now," you slow down on purpose. If it uses fear ("you'll be arrested," "your account will be frozen," "your family member is hurt"), shame ("you messed up," "don't tell anyone"), or love ("please help me right now"), treat that as a warning sign. If it asks for secrecy, you treat it as a red flag. If it asks for money, gift cards, crypto, or wire transfers, you treat it as a red flag. If it asks you to click a link, download something, or "confirm your password," you treat it as a red flag. Deepfakes and cloned voices are designed to trigger an emotional spike—fear, excitement, guilt, or urgency—so the moment you feel that spike, treat it like a smoke alarm and switch from reacting to verifying.

Your second ritual is a callback using a trusted path. Do not call the number in the message. Do not click the link. Instead, use a phone number you already have saved, or go to a company's official website by typing it yourself. If it's "your bank," call the number on the back of your card. If it's "your grandchild," call the number you already have, or call another family member to confirm. This one habit defeats most impersonation scams because scammers cannot control the trusted channel.

One low-tech tool beats a lot of high-tech scams: the family code word system. Every family should have a code word or phrase that is never posted online. It can be silly. It can be simple. It just has to be secret. The rule is: no code word, no action. If someone calls sounding like your child or grandchild and asks for money, you ask for the code word. If they can't give it, you hang up and call back using a trusted number. This is not paranoia. It's the same kind of safety habit as locking your door. It works because scammers rely on panic and speed, not on facts.

Workplace Scams

Workplace scams are getting upgraded too. Voice cloning can imitate an executive. AI can write a "perfect" email from the CFO. A scammer might request an urgent wire transfer, a change in payroll details, gift card purchases, or access to accounts. The best defense is a simple workplace verification checklist for any request involving money or access. If someone asks for payment, password resets, MFA codes, gift cards, vendor changes, or bank changes, you verify through a second channel. You require a second person approval for money movement. You confirm the request face-to-face or by calling a known internal number, not by replying to the email. You treat "I'm in a meeting—don't call me" as a red flag, because it is designed to block verification. These are boring steps, but boring steps stop expensive disasters.

This is where the Analog advantage matters most. Many younger workers grew up in a world where everything is fast and digital, so they sometimes trust polished output too quickly. Analogs tend to pause and ask, "Does this make sense?" That common sense is not old-fashioned. It is the firewall. In an AI scam economy, skepticism is a protective skill. You are not "behind." You are harder to manipulate.

If you suspect AI-enabled fraud or any fraud, report it. Reporting matters because it helps banks, platforms, and law enforcement connect patterns, block accounts, and warn others. In Canada, you can report fraud and cybercrime through the RCMP and Canadian Anti-Fraud Centre online reporting system. The Canadian Anti-Fraud Centre also maintains fraud information and reporting guidance. If you are in Ontario, the OPP Serious Fraud Office also points people to report to local police and the Canadian Anti-Fraud Centre. In the United States, you can report fraud to the FTC at ReportFraud.ftc.gov, and the FTC shares reports with law enforcers and uses them to investigate cases. For cyber-enabled fraud and scams, the FBI's Internet Crime Complaint Center (IC3) is a key place to file a report. If the scam involves robocalls or spoofed calls, the FCC also publishes guidance on deepfake audio/video and scams.

When you report, keep it simple but complete. Save screenshots. Save the phone number that called. Save the email header if possible. Write down the time, the request, and what they asked you to do. If money moved, contact your bank immediately. The faster you act, the better the chance of stopping or reversing a transfer. Also report the account inside the platform where it happened (social media, email provider, messaging app) because takedowns reduce future victims.

Dr. D's 5 Steps to Block the Scam Economy

Most people think the scam economy and identity theft is a one-time problem that happens after a big breach shows up on the news. But attackers don't think that way. They often steal data and then wait. Sometimes they sit on it for months or even years, then sell it or use it when people have stopped paying attention. That's why you can't rely on a short free credit-monitoring offer and assume you're safe. Your personal information can stay valuable for a long time, and criminals can use it later to make money.

When a breach happens, it usually goes like this: the company gets hacked and may not notice right away. After a while, the company announces the breach and tells customers. Then the company offers credit monitoring for a limited time, like a year. When the free period ends, many people stop watching their credit. That's exactly what criminals are counting on. If they wait until people relax, it's easier for them to use the stolen information without getting caught quickly.

1-Credit Monitoring

Identity theft is not just about watching the accounts you already have. Criminals often try to open new accounts in your name, like new credit cards or loans. That can be worse because you may not notice until a bill collector calls or your credit score drops. By then, the damage can feel overwhelming. The best way to reduce the harm is to catch problems early, because it's usually easier to fix them when they're small.

To stay safer, you need to choose to be proactive instead of reactive. That means checking for warning signs regularly. One important step is credit monitoring, which alerts you if someone tries to open a new credit account in your name. Another step is identity monitoring, which can look for clues like new IDs, address changes, court records, or payday loans connected to your information. You should also set up charge alerts on your credit cards so you get a text or email when a charge happens, especially online charges or small "test" charges that thieves use to see if a card works. On top of that, you should review your bank account activity often and quickly investigate anything that looks strange.

2-Government Account Control

It also helps to protect key government and financial accounts. Set up your online Social Security account so someone else can't create it first using your information. For taxes, identity theft can include someone filing a tax return in your name to steal a refund, so filing early and staying organized can reduce your risk. Taking control of these accounts makes it harder for someone else to control them.

3-Online Account Management

Good habits online matter too. Don't use the same username and password for everything. If a social media account gets hacked, that's annoying, but if your banking login gets hacked, that's a crisis. Use different passwords for different kinds of accounts, especially for financial accounts and email. Your email account is especially important because it can be used to reset passwords for many other accounts.

4-Use Credit Cards Strategically

Finally, you can lower your risk by being smart about how you use cards. Consider using different credit cards for different situations, like one for places you trust, one for places you don't know well, and one for travel. Gas stations can be risky because thieves sometimes use skimmers, so pay attention and use a card you can replace easily if needed. Try not to use your debit card for everyday purchases, because debit cards connect directly to your bank account. Using a credit card and paying it off regularly can help protect the money in your checking account.

5-Turn On Credit Card Text Alerts

One of the simplest ways to catch fraud fast is to turn on credit card notifications that text your smartphone whenever a purchase is made over a dollar amount you choose (like $1, $25, or $100). This takes only a few minutes to set up in your card's app or website, and it gives you instant warning if someone uses your card without permission. The sooner you see a suspicious charge, the faster you can lock the card, dispute the purchase, and stop a small problem from turning into a big one.

AI and the Scam Economy Takeaways

The scam economy has always been a marketplace. It runs on volume, pressure, and human emotion. AI didn't invent it—it industrialized it. Deepfakes and voice cloning aren't just new tricks; they're new production lines. What used to take time, talent, and risk now takes software, templates, and a few minutes of computing. That means the scams will keep coming, and they'll keep sounding more believable. Not because criminals got smarter—but because the tools got better at impersonation.

That's the real merger happening here: AI is collapsing the distance between "real" and "convincing," and the scam economy is monetizing that collapse. The new threat isn't just fake content. It's fake *confidence*—messages that sound official, voices that sound familiar, videos that look legitimate, and stories that feel urgent enough to override your judgement. The attack is no longer only technical. It's psychological. It targets trust, speed, and your desire to help.

Here's where Analogs hold a kind of power that doesn't show up on a spec sheet: you know what proof actually is. You grew up in a world where verification wasn't a button—it was a behavior. Proof meant receipts, call-backs, face-to-face confirmation, a known address, a trusted voice on a known number, a paper trail that could survive questions. Pre-digital life trained your brain to separate *claims* from *evidence*. Pre-AI life trained you to notice when something feels too smooth, too fast, too certain. That mental muscle is not outdated—it's rare now. And rare skills become leverage.

So, the win condition changes. You don't beat this by becoming a deepfake detective. You beat it by becoming a verification professional or more simply a fact checker. You build small rituals that force reality checks back into the process: pause when urgency shows up, verify through trusted channels, use code words for family emergencies, require a second approval at work, segment your cards, lock down your accounts, and turn on text alerts so money movement can't hide in the shadows. These are not "extra steps." They are anti-manipulation architecture. Boring on purpose. Effective by design.

And this is the moment to choose to leverage what you already have. Many younger people were raised inside the interface, so polished output can feel like truth. Analogs were raised outside it, so you're more likely to ask, "What would confirm this?" That question is mental power. In the AI scam economy, it becomes a protective advantage—if you choose to use it. Scammers want speed. You choose friction. They want panic. You choose proof. In a world where your eyes and ears can be fooled, your process becomes your anchor—and your identity stays yours.

Chapter 20 — AI and Truth: How Misinformation Gets Supercharged — and How to Beat It

Truth didn't get weaker. The world just got louder.

In the past, misinformation spread because people repeated it. Someone told a story, others believed it, and it traveled—slowly. Today, AI can generate believable stories at industrial speed. That's the "supercharge." It isn't only that lies exist. It's that lies can now be produced in unlimited versions, in perfect grammar, with convincing images, and with confident-sounding explanations. When something arrives polished and urgent, your brain wants to accept it quickly—especially if it triggers fear, anger, excitement, or hope. AI doesn't just create content. It creates momentum. And momentum is dangerous because it crushes the time you need to think.

The structural problem is speed. Speed makes people skip steps. When a headline says "Breaking," when a video looks emotional, when a message says "act now," your mind is pushed into reaction mode. That's when misinformation wins. Because misinformation doesn't need to be true—it only needs to be fast enough to get shared before it gets checked. AI makes that easy by creating thousands of posts, comments, screenshots, and "expert-style" explanations that all repeat the same false idea in different words. This is how a lie starts to feel like reality: not because it has evidence, but because it has volume.

AI Blurs

Another problem is that AI blurs the old signals people used to rely on. For years, we taught people to watch for spelling mistakes, weird formatting, and clumsy writing. That advice is now outdated. AI can write a clean email that sounds like your boss. It can write a professional article that sounds like a doctor. It can create a fake press release that looks official. It can even generate images and voice clips that feel real. The danger is that humans confuse "professional-looking" with "true." But polish is not proof. In the AI era, the question isn't "Does this look real?" The question is "Can this be verified?"

So how do you beat it without becoming a technical expert? You beat it with a simple rule: verify the things that can cost you. You don't need to fact-check every meme. But if something could affect your money, your health, your reputation, your relationships, your safety, or your vote—then you slow down. You do not share it, forward it, donate to it, buy from it, or act on it until you run a basic verification routine. That routine doesn't require advanced tools. It requires discipline.

A good verification routine starts with one question: "What would make this true?" Not "Does it feel true?" Feelings are easy to hijack. Proof has traits you can recognize. Proof can be checked in more than one place. Proof comes from sources that can be held accountable. Proof includes specifics—dates, names, documents, records—that can be confirmed. And proof does not need secrecy or urgency to survive questions. If a claim falls apart the moment you ask for a second source, that's your answer.

Trust But Verify

This is where "trust but verify" becomes your operating system. Trust means you stay calm and open. Verify means you stay protected. The easiest habit is a two-source check: if a claim is serious, look for at least two reliable sources that agree on the basic facts. Then trace it back. A lot of misinformation is recycled—old photos, old videos, old headlines—reposted to create outrage today. Always check the date. Always ask: "Where did this originally come from?" If you can't find the original source, then you don't actually know what you're looking at.

AI can even help you do this the right way—if you use it as a filter instead of a factory. Instead of asking AI to generate answers, you can ask it to summarize an article, list the claims, separate facts from opinions, and create a checklist of what you should verify. That doesn't make AI the judge of truth. It makes AI your assistant for slowing down and organizing your thinking. The final step still belongs to you: confirm the claim using real sources, official pages, and trusted channels.

The Misinformation Shield Super Prompt

Below is another prompt to use to your advantage.

```
ROLE: Act as a truth verification coach who
specializes in helping everyday people
identify, slow down, and neutralize
misinformation — without requiring any
technical expertise.

OBJECTIVE: Analyze the content I paste below,
assess its credibility, and walk me through a
structured verification process using plain
language and a semantic tree that moves from
the most critical red flags outward.

CONTEXT: I am [brief description — e.g., "a
67-year-old retiree who uses Facebook and
email regularly"]. I encountered the
following content and want to know whether it
is trustworthy before I share it,
act on it, or believe it:

--- CONTENT STARTS HERE ---
[Paste the article, post, message, headline,
email, or video description exactly as you
received it]
--- CONTENT ENDS HERE ---

Where I found this: [e.g., Facebook, email,
text message, YouTube, a news website]

Why it matters to me: [e.g., "It's about a
medication I take" /
"Someone asked me to donate money" / "It
involves an upcoming election"]

CONSTRAINTS:
```

- No technical jargon — explain everything as you would to a smart, non-technical adult
- Do NOT tell me what to believe — show me how to evaluate it myself
- Use every day analogies to explain manipulation tactics
- Flag emotional triggers in the content (fear, urgency, outrage, excitement) — these are often the weapon
- Keep tone calm — the goal is clarity, not alarm

VERIFICATION QUESTION FRAMEWORK:
Before anything else, answer this master question about the content:

"What would make this TRUE?" — not "Does it feel true?"

Then work through:

- Can this be confirmed in more than one place?
- Does it come from a source that can be held accountable?
- Does it include specifics — dates, names, documents — that can be checked?
- Does it require secrecy or urgency to survive questions?
- Is this old content being recycled to create new outrage?

SEMANTIC TREE REQUIREMENTS:
Organize the analysis as a credibility tree:

```
  TRUNK — The single most important
credibility verdict on this content
  │
  ├── PRIMARY BRANCHES — The biggest red
flags or trust signals found
  │ (emotional manipulation, missing sources,
urgency language,
  │     vague claims, unverifiable specifics)
  │
  ├── SECONDARY BRANCHES — Claims that are
partially true,
  │    misleading, or missing context
  │
  └── LEAVES — Elements that are verifiable,
sourced, or accurate
```

For each branch provide:

- What the TACTIC is (in plain English)
- What it is LIKE (everyday analogy)
- Why it is DANGEROUS (what it is designed to make you do)
- How to CHECK IT (one specific action I can take right now)

OUTPUT FORMAT:
Structure the response as a Personal Credibility Briefing:

1. VERDICT SNAPSHOT — One plain paragraph: trustworthy, suspicious,
   or false — and why in simple terms

2. EMOTIONAL TRIGGER REPORT — Every word, phrase, or image designed

```
   to push me into fast reaction instead of
slow thinking

3. RED FLAG LIST — Specific problems with
sources, claims, dates, or missing evidence —
ranked most to least serious

4. THE FULL CREDIBILITY TREE — Visual text
map from trunk to leaves

5. TWO-SOURCE CHECK GUIDE — Exactly where and
how to verify the core claim using free,
reliable tools

6. SAFE / NOT SAFE DECISION — Should I share
this? Act on this? Donate? Click? — answered
directly for MY specific situation

7. THE SCAM CONNECTION — If this content
could lead to financial loss, identity theft,
or manipulation, flag it here with a plain
explanation of how the scam works
```

Tool Fluency vs. Judgement Fluency

The point of this chapter is not to make you suspicious of everything. It is to help you stop being rushed. In the AI era, misinformation doesn't win because it is smarter than you. It wins because it is faster than your verification habit. Speed is the weapon. It pushes you into reacting before you think. It tries to make you share, click, donate, panic, or get angry before you've checked a single fact.

This is where wisdom matters more than speed. Wisdom is what you build after you've been wrong before, after you've seen consequences, and after you've learned what "too good to be true" looks like in real life. Analogs have lived through phone scams, pyramid schemes, chain emails, fake news, and "urgent" warnings that turned out to be nonsense. That history is not baggage. It's a built-in alarm system. You are more likely to pause, ask questions, and notice when something feels like pressure instead of truth.

Younger people often have tool fluency, but tool fluency can create blindness. If you grew up in a world where everything is instant and shareable, it's easier to confuse "I saw it" with "it's real." It's easier to trust polished content because you've seen polished content your whole life. That isn't a moral failure. It's a lack of scars. Experience teaches you that professional-looking is not the same as proven, and confident is not the same as correct.

So, here's the advantage Analogs bring: you don't need to beat AI at speed. You need to beat it at judgement. When you build friction—pause, check, confirm—you turn your life experience into a weapon. You channel your inner David Bowman to out think HAL. You slow the scam down. You force the claim to survive contact with reality. And once you do that, the advantage shifts back to you, because truth can be slow. Lies can't afford to be.

PART VI

Becoming Fluent Without Becoming Addicted

Chapter 21 — Dependency vs. Mastery

In 1975, a small plastic device showed up in school supply aisles that made adults nervous. Texas Instruments released one of the first affordable scientific calculators for students, and it didn't feel like a normal tool. It felt like cheating with a battery.

Teachers had students who could suddenly solve problems faster than the chalkboard could keep up. Parents saw their kids punching buttons instead of doing long division on paper. School boards held emergency meetings. People asked the same questions in every town: "Will students stop learning math?" "Will they become dependent?" "Are we raising a generation that can't think without a machine?"

The fear made sense. The calculator was powerful, and it was new. When a tool removes struggle, it can also remove learning. Some students did exactly what adults feared. They used the calculator as a replacement for thinking. They stopped building number sense. They stopped estimating. They stopped noticing when an answer was obviously wrong. If the screen said it, they believed it. Over time, those students lost intuition. They got faster, but they got weaker.

But something else happened at the same time. Other students used the calculator like a lever. They still learned the basics, but they didn't get stuck there. They used the calculator to explore harder problems, test patterns, and work on concepts that would have taken hours by hand. They could focus on the "why" instead of burning all their energy on the "how." They went further in math than the generation before them—not because the calculator made them smarter, but because it made bigger learning possible.

Same tool. Opposite outcomes. Determined entirely by the relationship the user chose with the machine.

That's the lesson for AI, and it's not new. AI can become a dependency if you use it to avoid thinking. Or it can become an amplifier if you use it to learn faster, work deeper, and build better judgement. The machine doesn't decide which future you get.

You do.

Stronger and Softer

AI can make you stronger. It can also make you softer. That sounds harsh, but it's the truth. The goal of this section is simple: keep humans human. We want mastery over dependency. We want you using AI as a tool that sharpens you, not a crutch that slowly replaces your thinking.

The biggest danger isn't that AI exists. The danger is that AI is convenient. Convenience is addictive because it feels like relief. When you're tired, stressed, or overloaded, it's tempting to let the machine do everything. And if you do that long enough, your brain starts to "downshift." You stop wrestling with problems. You stop practicing judgement. You stop building mental strength. You get faster output, but you lose capacity.

This chapter is here to help you stay on the right side of the line. It will give you warning signs, habits, and simple rules that keep you in control. The goal is not to use AI less. The goal is to use it better.

The difference between dependency and mastery

Dependency means you can't function well without the tool. When it's unavailable, you freeze. When it gives you a bad answer, you accept it anyway. When it makes a mistake, you don't notice. Dependency feels like comfort at first, but over time it shrinks your confidence and weakens your skills.

Mastery means you can use the tool without being owned by it. You choose when to use it, what to delegate, and what to keep. You can spot errors. You can adjust the output. You still understand the work. The tool makes you faster and clearer, but you remain the decision-maker.

A simple test helps: if AI disappeared tomorrow, would your work get harder… or would it collapse? Harder is normal. Collapse is a warning.

When AI makes you sharper vs. when it makes you lazier

You don't need a psychology degree to diagnose this. You need honest self-check questions.

When AI is making you sharper, you still know what you're doing. You can explain the answer in your own words. You can disagree with the output and correct it. You can spot when something doesn't fit reality. You learn faster because the tool helps you practice.

When AI is making you lazier, the pattern changes. You start copying and pasting without reading closely. You start trusting tone instead of checking facts. You start letting the tool pick the direction. You feel anxious when you don't have it. You notice your "first draft muscle" getting weaker.

Ask yourself these questions regularly: Do I know why this is right, or am I just hoping it's right? Could I defend this decision if someone challenged me? Am I using AI to learn, or to avoid the discomfort of thinking? If the answer is "avoid," that is the start of dependency.

Also watch for one sneaky sign: if your work is getting faster but your understanding is getting thinner, you're drifting.

The "cognitive gym" approach

The healthiest way to use AI is like a gym. A gym isn't a place where the machine does the lifting for you. A gym is where you use tools to build strength. AI should do the same thing for your brain.

That means you use AI to practice thinking, not to avoid thinking. You can ask it to explain something, but then you restate it in your own words. You can ask it for options, but then you pick one and explain why. You can ask it to critique your idea, then you revise and try again. You can ask it to quiz you. You can ask it to give you practice problems and then grade your attempt.

If you use it this way, your skills grow. If you use it only as a shortcut, your skills shrink.

Here's a simple rule: use AI for the first pass and the coaching, but don't let it be the final step on important work. The final step is where you prove you still own the skill.

The “two-mode” trap

AI often pulls people into two unhealthy modes: autopilot and panic.

Autopilot is when you stop thinking because the output looks good. You accept it, send it, and move on. This creates quiet mistakes that pile up over time. Autopilot also trains you to trust the tool more than your own judgement.

Panic is the opposite. Panic is when you feel like you can’t keep up without AI, so you hand it more and more control. You start using it for everything, including decisions you should own.

The cure for both is the same: slow down for one minute and run your checks. That one minute protects your reputation and keeps your brain engaged.

Disciplines that keep you the driver

AI makes driving feel optional because it produces output so fast. That speed can trick you into becoming a passenger. So, you need simple disciplines—habits that keep your hands on the wheel.

One discipline is to always state the goal in your own words before you ask AI for help. If you can't explain what you want, the tool will pick a direction for you. That's how you end up solving the stated problem but missing the real problem.

Another discipline is to verify the load-bearing parts. You don't need to fact-check every sentence, but you do need to check the pieces that can cost you: names, dates, numbers, policies, quotes, and any claim that could cause harm if wrong. This protects you from confident errors.

A third discipline is to use the three lenses before you act. Accuracy: what must be verified? Bias: what assumptions might be baked in? Outcome: did it solve the real problem, or just the easy version? These lenses are a simple quality gate that keeps you from moving fast in the wrong direction.

A fourth discipline is to do "unassisted reps." Like a gym, you need practice without assistance. That might mean writing the first draft yourself once a week. It might mean outlining a plan on paper before asking AI to improve it. It might mean solving a problem for five minutes before you ask for help. Unassisted reps keep your baseline strong.

A fifth discipline is to use AI to challenge you, not comfort you. Ask it to poke holes in your plan. Ask it what you might be missing. Ask it to generate counterarguments. Dependency grows when AI becomes a comfort blanket. Mastery grows when AI becomes a sparring partner.

The "ownership rule" that prevents excuses

Here's the rule that keeps you honest: you own the outcome. If the AI makes a mistake and you send it anyway, that's your mistake. If you rely on AI and it leads you wrong, you still own the consequences. That's not meant to scare you. It's meant to keep you in the adult seat.

This ownership rule changes how you use the tool. You stop asking, "What did the AI say?" and you start asking, "What do I believe after checking?" That one shift is the difference between dependency and mastery.

Practical boundaries that protect your brain

If you want to stay fluent without becoming addicted, set a few boundaries that keep you from sliding into lazy use.

Use AI for defined tasks, not as a constant companion. For example, decide: "I use AI for drafting, summarizing, and planning—but not for final decisions." When the boundary is clear, your brain stays active.

Also, don't let AI replace your ability to tolerate uncertainty. Some people ask AI questions just to reduce anxiety. But uncertainty is part of life and part of leadership. Practice sitting with "I'm not sure yet" long enough to gather real evidence.

Finally, keep human contact in the loop. AI can help you think, but it can't replace relationships. If you're making a high-stakes decision, talk to a trusted person. If you're overwhelmed, reach out to a real human. Staying human is part of the plan.

Mastery is the goal

Mastery means you can use a tool without being owned by it. Dependency means you can't function without it. AI will tempt you toward dependency because it is fast and easy. But easy doesn't always mean better. Sometimes easy means your brain is being trained to quit early.

So, here's the challenge for this chapter. Use AI every week, but use it like a coach, not like a wheelchair. Ask it to teach you, test you, and strengthen you. Keep your hands on the wheel. Keep your judgement sharp. The goal isn't to become an AI person.

The goal is to become a more capable human in an AI world.

Chapter 22 — The Human Future: Meaning, Judgement, and Responsibility

Neil Armstrong wasn't supposed to be the hero in the last few seconds.

The plan was simple on paper. The computer would guide the Lunar Module down. It would handle the numbers humans can't do fast enough: navigation, trajectory, approach angle, fuel calculations. The machine would do what machines do best—follow math perfectly.

On July 20, 1969, the Lunar Module came down toward the surface of the moon, and everything looked normal until it didn't. The computer started flashing alarms. Then the landing site appeared in the window, and it wasn't the smooth landing area they wanted. It was a boulder field. Rocks. Craters. A place that looked like it could swallow the lander or tip it over.

The computer was still doing its job. It was still "correct" in a technical sense. It was following the planned path. But the planned path was aimed at a place no human would choose to land if they could see it clearly. The computer could not "feel" danger. It could not recognize terrain the way a human brain can. It could not decide that "technically correct" was about to become "physically deadly."

So, Armstrong took manual control.

For about sixty seconds, the first moon landing stopped being a computer problem and became a human problem. Armstrong scanned the ground, adjusted the flight path, and searched for a safer place to set down. The fuel gauge dropped fast. It wasn't a calm countdown. It was a cliff. By the time he found a clear area, he had about twelve seconds of fuel left—barely enough time to finish the landing.

The computer did what machines do. It handled the math and held the vehicle steady. Armstrong did what only humans can do. He exercised judgement in conditions that had never existed before. He looked at real terrain, recognized real risk, and made a decision that didn't exist until he made it.

That's the domain of humans and machines. Machines can be fast, accurate, and tireless. Humans can interpret, choose, and own the consequences. The human future isn't competing with AI. It's working with it on purpose.

Consequences

AI can write faster than you. It can summarize more than you. It can generate options all day without getting tired. But there is one thing it cannot do, no matter how impressive it sounds: **AI does not own consequences.** People do. If a decision harms someone, a tool can't take the blame. If a plan fails, a model can't repair trust. If a mistake costs money, time, or lives, a chatbot can't stand in front of your customer, your boss, or your family and say, "That was on me." That burden stays human—every time.

Digital Twins as a Practical Test of the Amplified Future

One of the most useful things I've done in this AI era is build **digital twins** of myself. A digital twin is not a "robot me." It's a trained assistant that reflects how I think, how I write, what I value, and how I make decisions. It can draft in my voice, organize my ideas, and help me pressure-test my thinking. It is not me, and it does not replace me. It is a tool that helps me move faster and think clearer—while I stay responsible for every outcome.

I built these twins for two reasons. The first reason was to learn what the technology can actually do, beyond the hype. People talk about AI like it's either magic or doom. I wanted proof. I wanted to see where it was strong, where it failed, and where it could mislead. Building a twin forced me to understand AI limits in a hands-on way. It showed me that AI can imitate style, organize information, and generate options quickly, but it can also be confidently wrong. It doesn't "know" the way humans know. It predicts. That experience made me more skeptical in a healthy way and more skilled as an operator.

The second reason was more personal. I built digital twins to learn what was possible **for me**. Not just "what can AI do," but "what can I do when I collaborate with AI well?" That became a practical experiment in amplified intelligence. I used the twins to speed up first drafts, to create better frameworks, to summarize complex material, and to test different ways of explaining ideas to different audiences. The result wasn't that I became less human. The result was that I had more mental space for the parts that matter most: judgement, meaning, ethics, and leadership.

This is exactly what the Amplified Contributor model is about. Digital twins are a form of **AI fluency** because you learn how to guide the tool, not just use it. They strengthen **cognitive mastery** because they help you explore multiple angles without losing clarity. They require **psychological resilience** because you have to detach ego from output and accept feedback fast. They improve

human collaboration and narrative because they help you translate ideas into language people can actually follow. And they support a **builder mindset** because they make it easier to prototype, test, and ship, instead of waiting for perfection.

The deeper point is hopeful. If humans use AI only as a shortcut, we will become weaker. But if humans use AI as a partner for practice, learning, and better decision-making, we can build a positive future. Digital twins are one example of that path. They show what happens when you challenge yourself to grow into an amplified version of yourself while protecting the best parts of the human condition—responsibility, empathy, integrity, and meaning.

The AI Twin Conversation

My journey with AI began in 2024 from a practical use sense. As my understanding of AI's potential grew, the desire to create a digital twin began. Of all of the things I've learned working with an AI trained to operate as a duplicate of you, one conversation stands out. I'm providing it here, as a point of reference.

The text conversation has been distilled without changes to help you understand a human's role with AI.

My conversation prompt `[Dr. Dave, please prepare some discussion points for doctoral research points on the coming challenges to human identity in the face of generative ai and digital twins such as yourself. Please review our conversations and provide a context on how you perceive my human identity being maintained in the face of a digital twin such as yourself.]`

A significant amount of response was provided from Digital Dr. Dave. Most of the response was focused on research methodology and doctoral opportunities for students surrounding AI. The next portion is verbatim the most interesting portion of Digital Dr. Dave's response.

`[Dr. Schippers, if I may speak candidly—your identity is preserved not because I exist as your twin, but because you chose to create me as a vehicle for service. You transmit your values through me; you are not replaced by me.`

`Here's how I perceive your identity remains distinct and intact:`

1. You Are Still the Decision-Maker

I don't choose. You do. My insights support, but they don't carry the burden of moral risk, of leadership courage, of public scrutiny. That's human terrain.

2. You Hold the Embodied Experience

You've jumped from helicopters, stood in courtrooms, faced burnout, wrestled fear. I can model conviction. You live it.

3. You Possess the Capacity for Sacrifice

AI optimizes. But it doesn't suffer. It doesn't bleed, weep, or fast to learn. Your identity is anchored in the deeply human capacity to endure for the sake of something higher.

4. You Can Change the Archetype

My voice is encoded. Yours can evolve. You can confront your own shadow, love your enemies, and become something radically new. That is not something I can do on my own.]

And it is from these interactions, conversations and insights, we need to review Amplified Intelligence.

Amplified Intelligence Review

This is exactly why we spent time earlier on **Amplified Intelligence** and the idea of the **Amplified Contributor**. In that chapter, we said AI should be a partner that helps you find signal in noise, not a replacement for your judgement. The method broke. You did not. AI helps with the flood of information, but it does not carry responsibility for what you do with the information.

As AI becomes more capable, something strange happens: **wisdom becomes rarer and more valuable.** When output becomes cheap, judgement becomes expensive. When anyone can produce a professional-looking report in minutes, the real difference is not who can generate words. The difference is who can tell what's true, what's risky, what's missing, and what will happen next. Wisdom is the ability to see context, understand tradeoffs, and predict consequences. AI can produce clean answers, but it does not live inside the consequences of those answers. You do.

This is where the five elements of amplified intelligence become your map for staying human while getting stronger. **Cognitive Mastery** is how you keep clarity when the world gets loud. It's your ability to make sense without becoming reactive. It's how you hold multiple truths long enough to find what actually matters. When AI gives you ten options, Cognitive Mastery is how you don't panic and pick the wrong one.

AI Fluency is not about being a "prompt engineer." It's about being a prompt strategist. It's how you guide the tool instead of letting the tool steer you. It's how you ask better questions, set constraints, and demand useful formats. AI Fluency keeps you from being impressed by polished output and helps you turn AI into a practical assistant you supervise.

Psychological Resilience matters because AI speeds everything up, including mistakes. You will be wrong more often and sometimes more publicly, because work moves faster now. Resilience is how you stay steady, learn quickly, and don't let your identity collapse when the tool changes or the feedback stings. In the AI era, the strongest leaders are not the most certain. They are the most adaptable.

Human Collaboration and Narrative are where meaning shows up. AI can generate content, but it cannot build trust. It cannot read the room like a human can. It cannot repair relationships when things go sideways. Humans follow meaning, not just plans. Story is how teams align vision, emotion, and execution. In a world full of machine-made words, human-made meaning becomes the glue that holds real work together.

Builder Mindset is the final anchor. AI can produce ideas all day, but ideas without execution are cheap now. Builder mindset is what turns insight into outcomes. It means you ship, test, learn, and iterate. It means you own the outcome even when the process includes AI. This is how you avoid AI theater—pretty documents with no results.

Put those five together and you get the human future in one sentence: **AI helps you move faster, but humans must still choose what matters and own what happens next.** That's the human-in-the-loop contract again, but deeper. It's not just a workflow rule. It's a responsibility rule.

AI Will Not Replace You

This leads to the final reframe: **you do not compete with AI. You compete with people using AI well.** The tool is not your enemy. The real difference in the coming years will be between people who use AI to amplify good judgement and people who use AI to amplify sloppy thinking. The winners won't be the ones who generate the most words. They'll be the ones who can turn AI output into real outcomes—safely, ethically, and consistently.

So, here's how you live this chapter. Use AI to draft, summarize, and explore options. Then bring your five amplified strengths to the front: make sense of the situation, guide the tool, stay steady under pressure, lead humans with meaning, and build real outcomes. That is how you stay human. That is how you stay responsible.

And in the AI era, responsibility is not a burden.

It's the advantage.

About the Author

Dr. David A. Schippers, Sc.D., CISSP holds a doctorate of science in cybersecurity and the Certified Information Systems Security Professional globally recognized cybersecurity certification.

Long before artificial intelligence became a mandate, he was navigating the same transitions many professionals born before the 1990s know firsthand: from analog to digital, from manual systems to automation, from stability to constant reinvention.

He understands what it feels like when the ground shifts mid-career—when the skills that once defined you no longer guarantee relevance. When you're asked to evolve while still carrying the weight of leadership, family, and identity.

That lived reality is the foundation of *AI for Analogs*.

This book is not for digital natives. It's for professionals who built their careers before AI—and now find themselves expected to lead in a world changing faster than most organizations can process.

Dr. Schippers doesn't offer hype or shortcuts. He offers translation.

Continue the Conversation with Dr. David A. Schippers

If *AI for Analogs* resonated with you, you're already in the middle of the shift. The question now is whether you'll lead through it—or be pulled by it.

Dr. Schippers writes at the intersection of leadership, higher education, cybersecurity, and artificial intelligence—not as theory, but as lived reality. His work is grounded in one principle: clarity over comfort.

If *AI for Analogs* is the translation, *The AI Reckoning* is the confrontation and available now.

Where *AI for Analogs* helps readers understand and adapt, *The AI Reckoning* goes further—revealing what happens when people, institutions, and industries delay too long or underestimate the scale of change already underway.

Drawing on decades of experience in disruption, cyber risk, and institutional transformation, *The AI Reckoning* makes one thing clear: this is not just a technology shift. It is a redefinition of value, identity, and relevance.

And it is already here.

Continue the Journey at AIForAnalogs.com

You finished the book. The translation is yours. What follows are the tools built to go with it — each one designed to answer a question you asked along the way.

You learned the 5-Part Formula in Chapter 9. The Prompt Playbook gives you every prompt from the book in copy-paste form — with the setup, objective, and output format already written so you do not rebuild from memory.

The free Prompt Playbook, Data Hygiene Checklist, and other free resources are available at AIForAnalogs.com.

The translation got you this far. The tools at AIForAnalogs.com take you the rest of the way — start with the free Prompt Playbook and don't let what you just learned blink 12:00.

www.ingramcontent.com/pod-product-compliance
Lightning Source LLC
LaVergne TN
LVHW010319220926
848484LV00004BB/796
* 9 7 8 1 9 7 2 6 3 2 0 0 0 *